EDINBURGH

Contents

INTRODUCTION 8

THE MAGIC OF EDINBURGH 13
Edinburgh Castle by Night 14
Silhouette of Edinburgh from Calton Hill 15
Arthur's Seat 16
The Pentland Hills 18
Bass Rock 19
Fireworks 20
Statues in Waverley Market 21
Clock Tower 22
Fidra Lighthouse 24
Poppy Fields, Dunbar 25

TRADITION & ENTERTAINMENT 26
Ghost Tours 28
Ross Open Air Theatre 29
Edinburgh Festival Fringe 30
Edinburgh International Festival 31
Military Tattoo 32
Scots Guard 33
Traverse Theatre 34
Festival Theatre 35
Usher Hall 36
Royal Highland Show 38
Edinburgh Zoo 39
One O'Clock Gun, Edinburgh Castle 40
Procession, Royal Mile 41
Playhouse Theatre 42
Museum of Childhood 43

KIRKS & CATHEDRALS 44
St Mary's Episcopalian Cathedral 46
Aerial View, St Mary's Episcopalian Cathedral 47
St John's Kirk 48
Dalmeny Kirk 49
St Mary's Church, Haddington 50
St Andrew and St George's 52

Tron Kirk 53
St Margaret's Chapel, Edinburgh Castle 54
Canongate Kirk 55
Apprentice Pillar, Rosslyn Chapel 56
St Anthony's Chapel 57
St Cuthbert's Kirk 58
Corstorphine Church 60
Greyfriars Kirkyard 61
High Kirk of St Giles 62
Thistle Chapel, High Kirk of St Giles 63

LIFE & CULTURE 64
Scotch Whisky Heritage Centre 66
Royal Museum of Scotland 67
Parliament Square 68
Waverley Station 69
Old Observatory, Calton Hill 70
Camera Obscura 71
The City Chambers 72
Register House 73
Edinburgh International Conference Centre 74
Royal Bank of Scotland 76
West Register House 77
National Gallery of Scotland 78
Divinity College, Edinburgh University 79
Murrayfield Stadium 80
Meadowbank Stadium 81
Braid Hill Golf Course 82
Balmoral Hotel 83

THE OLD & THE NEW 84
The New Town 86
The Old Town 87
Victoria Street 88
White Horse Close 89
Moray Place 90
St Andrew's Square 91
Castlehill, The Royal Mile 92
The Mound 93
North Bridge 94
Tenement Housing, Marchmont 95
Fan Window, The New Town 97

The Royal Mile 98
Princes Street 99
Mylne's Court 100
Charlotte Square 101
Ramsay Garden 102
Ann Street 103

PARKS & WATERS 104
Princes Street Gardens 106
The Floral Clock 107
Dunsapie Loch 108
Newhaven Fishmarket 109
The Firth of Forth 110
Royal Botanic Garden 112
The Glasshouse, Royal Botanic Garden 113
Duddingston Loch 114
Holyrood Park 115
St Bernard's Well 116
The Meadows 117
Smug Anchorage, Cramond 118
St Margaret's Loch 120
Musselburgh Harbour 121
The Port of Leith 122
Union Canal 123

STATUES & MONUMENTS 124
National Monument, Calton Hill 126
Memorial to the Royal Scots Greys 127
Nelson Monument, Calton Hill 128
The Mercat Cross 129
Dugald Stewart Monument, Calton Hill 130
Greyfriars Bobby 132
Ross Fountain 133
Sherlock Holmes Statue 134
The Scott Monument 135
Burns Monument 136
Statue of George IV 138
Memorial Cannon, Calton Hill 139
Statue of Allan Ramsay 140
Statue of Field Marshal Haig 141

CASTLES & STATELY HOMES 142
The Palace of Holyroodhouse 144
Carving, Palace of Holyroodhouse 145
Lauriston Castle 146
Stevenson House 147
Tantallon Castle 148
Dirleton Castle 149
Blackness Castle 150
Craigmillar Castle 152
Dalmeny House 153
Edinburgh Castle, Spring 154
Penicuik House 155
Hopetoun House 156
Linlithgow Palace 157

HISTORIC EDINBURGH 158
Gladstone's Land 160
Holyrood Abbey 161
Edinburgh Castle, Late Afternoon 162
The Honours of Scotland, Edinburgh Castle 163
Roman Fort, Cramond 164
Old Royal High School 165
Grassmarket 166
Robert Louis Stevenson's House, Heriot Row 167
The Heart of Midlothian 168
Waterloo Bridge 170
John Knox's House 171
Canongate Tolbooth (The People's Story) 172
Inchcolm Abbey 173
Lady Stair's House (The Writer's Museum) 174
Deacon Brodie's Tavern 175
Gillespie Plaque 176
Huntly House Museum 177

AROUND EDINBURGH 178
Swanston Village 180
Inveresk Village 181
Dean Village 182
Stenton Village 183
Preston Mill, East Linton 184
Portobello Beach 186
Gifford Village 187
Dirleton Village 188
The Colonies, Stockbridge 189
Inn at Cramond 190
Hawes Inn, South Queensferry 192
Culross Village 193
Forth Road Bridge 194
Forth Rail Bridge 195

EDINBURGH PAST & PRESENT 196

INDEX 198

Contents by Region

The Royal Mile

Edinburgh Castle by Night	14
Fireworks	20
Ghost Tours	28
Edinburgh Festival Fringe	30
Edinburgh International Festival	31
Military Tattoo	32
Scots Guard	33
One O'Clock Gun, Edinburgh Castle	40
Procession, Royal Mile	41
Museum of Childhood	43
Tron Kirk	53
St Margaret's Chapel, Edinburgh Castle	54
Canongate Kirk	55
High Kirk of St Giles	62
Thistle Chapel, High Kirk of St Giles	63
Scotch Whisky Heritage Centre	66
Parliament Square	68
Camera Obscura	71
City Chambers	72
The Old Town	87
White Horse Close	89
Castlehill, The Royal Mile	92
The Royal Mile	98
Ramsay Garden	102

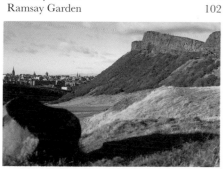

Mylne's Court	100
The Mercat Cross	129
Statue of Field Marshal Haig	141
The Palace of Holyroodhouse	144
Carving, Palace of Holyroodhouse	145
Edinburgh Castle, Spring	154
Holyrood Abbey	161
Lady Stair's House (The Writer's Museum)	174
Gladstone's Land	160
Gillespie Plaque	176
John Knox's House	171
Edinburgh Castle, Late Afternoon	162
The Honours of Scotland, Edinburgh Castle	163
Huntly House Museum	177
Canongate Tolbooth (The People's Story)	172
Deacon Brodie's Tavern	175
The Heart of Midlothian	168

Southern Edinburgh

Traverse Theatre	34
Festival Theatre	35
Usher Hall	36
Greyfriars Kirkyard	61
Royal Museum of Scotland	67
Edinburgh International Conference Centre	74
Divinity College, Edinburgh University	79
Victoria Street	88
Tenement Housing, Marchmont	96
The Meadows	117
Greyfriars Bobby	132
Grassmarket	166

The New Town

Edinburgh from Calton Hill	15
Statues in Waverley Market	21
Clock Tower, Princes Street	22
Ross Open Air Theatre	29
Playhouse Theatre	42
St Mary's Episcopal Cathedral	46
Aerial View, St Mary's Episcopal Cathedral	47
St John's Kirk	48
St Andrew and St George's	52
St Cuthbert's Kirk	58
Waverley Station	69
Old Observatory, Calton Hill	70
Register House	73
Royal Bank of Scotland	76
West Register House	77
National Gallery of Scotland	78
Balmoral Hotel	83
The New Town	86
Moray Place	90
St Andrew's Square	91
North Bridge	94
Fan Window, New Town	97
Princes Street	99
Charlotte Square	101

The Mound	93
Princes Street Gardens	106
The Floral Clock	107
National Monument, Calton Hill	126
Memorial to the Royal Scots Greys	127
Nelson Monument, Calton Hill	128
Dugald Stewart Monument, Calton Hill	130
Ross Fountain	133
Sherlock Holmes Statue	134
The Scott Monument	135
Burns Monument	136
Statue of George IV	138
Memorial Cannon, Calton Hill	139
Statue of Allan Ramsay	140
Old Royal High School	165
Robert Louis Stevenson's House, Heriot Row	167
Waterloo Bridge	170

The Suburbs

Arthur's Seat	16
Edinburgh Zoo	39
Royal Highland Show	38
Dalmeny Kirk	49
Corstorphine Church	60
St Anthony's Chapel, Holyrood Park	57
Murrayfield Stadium	80
Meadowbank Stadium	81
Ann Street, Stockbridge	103
Dunsapie Loch, Holyrood Park	108
Newhaven Fishmarket	109
Royal Botanic Garden	112
Glasshouse, Royal Botanic Garden	113
Duddingston Loch, Holyrood Park	114
Holyrood Park	115
St Bernard's Well, Dean Village	116
Smug Anchorage, Cramond	118
St Margaret's Loch, Holyrood Park	120
Musselburgh Harbour	121

The Port of Leith	122
Lauriston Castle	146
Craigmillar Castle	152
Dalmeny House	153
Hopetoun House	156
Roman Fort, Cramond	164
Inchcolm Abbey	173
Dean Village	182
Portobello Beach	186
The Colonies, Stockbridge	189
Inn at Cramond	190
Hawes Inn, South Queensferry	192
Forth Road Bridge	194
Forth Rail Bridge	195

Edinburgh Environs

The Pentland Hills	18
Bass Rock	19
Fidra Lighthouse	24
Poppy Fields, Dunbar	25
St Mary's Church, Haddington	50
Apprentice Pillar, Rosslyn Chapel	56
Braid Hill Golf Course	82
The Firth of Forth	110
Union Canal	123
Stevenson House	147
Tantallon Castle	148
Dirleton Castle	149
Blackness Castle	150
Penicuik House	155
Linlithgow Palace	157
Swanston Village	180
Inveresk Village	181
Stenton Village	183
Preston Mill, East Linton	184
Gifford Village	187
Dirleton Village	188
Culross Village	193

INTRODUCTION

Edinburgh is a city of contrasts: its diversity of character, landscape, architecture and history combine to make it a truly magical and unique place. The city's origins are ancient: archaeological evidence suggests that settlements existed on the formidable Castle Rock thousands of years BC, and since this time, Edinburgh has slowly expanded its boundaries, embracing a variety of characteristics that reflect every age which has contributed to the capital's rich and dramatic history.

The name 'Edinburgh' is believed to derive from the sixth-century settlement name 'Dun Eidyn', meaning 'Fort of Edin', and in its time this settlement marked the boundary between Scotland and England. The most significant moment in Edinburgh's history, however, really lies in the foundation of the castle in the eleventh century, for it was around this time that the city began to grow and prosper. Since its first stones were laid the castle has been the main focus of the city. Its importance has not diminished in nearly 900 years, and the castle's significance is as strong today as it was in ancient times – it is the symbol of Scotland's capital.

Like most capital cities, Edinburgh's fortunes have fluctuated over the centuries, and the city has witnessed some of Scotland's finest hours and darkest days. During the twelfth century, as the castle expanded and the abbey was founded at Holyrood, a town began to develop along what is now known as the Royal Mile, and by the mid-fifteenth century, the town had been granted a charter and was surrounded by its own walls. These would be needed, for Edinburgh became the focus of numerous attacks – political, religious and territorial – largely from the ever-present enemy to the south: England.

The English victory at the Battle of Flodden in 1513 was the start of hard times for Edinburgh. Determined to gain permanent rule over the Scots, the English monarchs sought unions with the Scottish royals. Mary, Queen of Scots, fled to France in an attempt to escape a union with the young Prince Edward, Henry VIII's only son. She returned in 1561 to a country rife with religious dissension and turmoil. A devout Catholic herself, Mary came into conflict on a number of occasions with the minister of

St Giles, John Knox – a Protestant reformer who, having spent some time exiled in Europe, had been strongly influenced by Calvinist ideals, and was now preaching these reforms to a responsive Edinburgh population. The tide of reform was too strong for Mary to turn back, and her downfall was tragic, but absolute. Her overthrow led eventually to a change in Edinburgh's role as capital, when her son James VI became James I of England on the death of Elizabeth I, uniting the thrones of the former enemies and moving the seat of the monarchy to London.

The century that followed was characterised by a series of religious struggles initiated by the introduction of Episcopacy to Scotland. This move, instigated by Charles I, was vastly unpopular in the north, and the aptly named 'killing times' ensued. It was at this time that the signing of the National Covenant took place at Greyfriars, and the subsequent rebellions meant persecution, imprisonment and death for many. Episcopacy was eventually overthrown – and the king executed – and the Presbyterian sect began to gain momentum. To this day it remains the main

religious following in Scotland. Edinburgh subsequently survived Oliver Cromwell and his armies and the Restoration, but with the Act of Union in 1707, the city's importance once again declined.

The tide of the Industrial Revolution brought about a turn in Edinburgh's fortunes, and although the city itself avoided succumbing completely to industry, in the way many northern cities did, the arrival of the railroads and other conveniences enhanced and broadened the professional opportunities that had previously been limited. The Age of Enlightenment burned bright in Scotland's capital city, as huge steps were taken in scientific and medical research, helped by the old and well-renowned university. The changes in art, architecture and literature manifested themselves in the very heart and soul of the city and the eighteenth and nineteenth centuries were acknowledged as Edinburgh's heyday. Some of the city's pre-eminent citizens hail from this period – architects, designers, sculptors, novelists and poets. The conception, and eventual creation, of the New Town epitomises the prosperity and magnificence of this era.

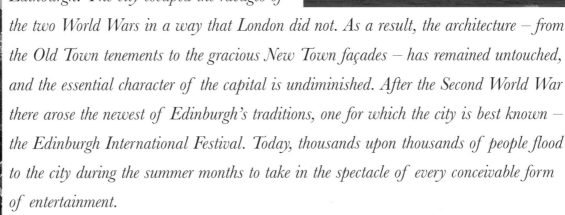

Recent history has been kind to Edinburgh. The city escaped the ravages of

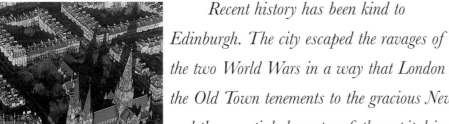

the two World Wars in a way that London did not. As a result, the architecture – from the Old Town tenements to the gracious New Town façades – has remained untouched, and the essential character of the capital is undiminished. After the Second World War there arose the newest of Edinburgh's traditions, one for which the city is best known – the Edinburgh International Festival. Today, thousands upon thousands of people flood to the city during the summer months to take in the spectacle of every conceivable form of entertainment.

Every step one takes through the streets of Edinburgh echoes this rich and fascinating history. The slabs of the Grassmarket cry out with the blood of the martyred Covenanters; the crowded closes along the Royal Mile reverberate with the hubbub of the

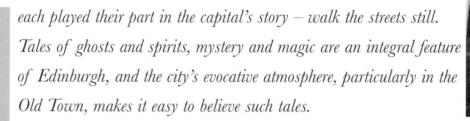

densely populated seventeenth-century Old Town; the sweeping avenues and carefully planned squares of James Craig's New Town reek of Georgian elegance and luxury. The people – rich and poor, kings and paupers, merchants and criminals – who have

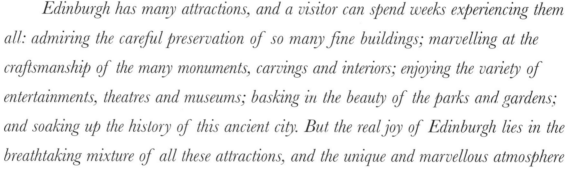

each played their part in the capital's story – walk the streets still. Tales of ghosts and spirits, mystery and magic are an integral feature of Edinburgh, and the city's evocative atmosphere, particularly in the Old Town, makes it easy to believe such tales.

Edinburgh has many attractions, and a visitor can spend weeks experiencing them all: admiring the careful preservation of so many fine buildings; marvelling at the craftsmanship of the many monuments, carvings and interiors; enjoying the variety of entertainments, theatres and museums; basking in the beauty of the parks and gardens; and soaking up the history of this ancient city. But the real joy of Edinburgh lies in the breathtaking mixture of all these attractions, and the unique and marvellous atmosphere

they combine to create here. Somehow, despite the diversity of style and structure, the city maintains a harmonious feel. The city has grown from small and humble roots, spread out geographically and boomed in terms of population. The modern and the ancient are embraced in Edinburgh in a welcoming and unconcerned manner. Nothing seems out of place. Even the sprawling Old Town has its own peculiar symmetry. There is a tale to tell on every corner and there is a welcome at every turn. The pleasure that can be gained from a visit to Scotland's magical capital, an exploration of its beautiful suburbs or a trip out into the beauty of the surrounding Lothian countryside, is inescapable and intoxicating.

THE MAGIC OF EDINBURGH

The magic of Edinburgh is evident at every turn: its great history, its diversity of architecture, its verdant parks and tranquil waters, all combine to create the unique and enchanting atmosphere that embraces this breathtaking city.

Edinburgh Castle
CASTLEHILL

The castle is the most impressive and mysterious feature of this ancient city. There have been settlements on Castle Rock – a craggy outcrop from an extinct volcano – from the earliest times. It is even possible that Stone Age men gathered here up to 8,000 years ago, hunting in the dense woods that long ago covered the whole of Edinburgh. Archaeological evidence dating from the Bronze Age – around 1000 BC – has been found, when it is believed people first lived on the rock.

Over the centuries the castle has grown, been fortified, destroyed and rebuilt on numerous occasions, but has remained the focal point of the city since it was first built. From the highest points of the castle, the rich and varied Scottish landscape stretches out for miles, encompassing rolling hills and dark crags, busy towns and quiet hamlets, valleys and rivers. From here, the threat of enemy attack could be spotted many miles distant and prepared for – its situation on the peak of the sheer cliff face being its most reliable defence. From anywhere in the city, the castle can be seen in all its ancient mystery and glory.

Silhouette of Edinburgh
FROM CALTON HILL

The views from the top of Calton Hill are more all-encompassing than from anywhere else, especially if one climbs to the highest viewpoint –the top of the Nelson Monument. The Firth of Forth stretches away to the north and east; to the south lies the dark roofs of the Old Town, the verdant Holyrood Park and the un-mistakable outcrop of the Salisbury Crags; in the west the lively bustle of the New Town is visible, and high on the ridge the castle, dark and brooding, surveys its kingdom.

Like the other hills in the area, Calton is part of Edinburgh's volcanic legacy, and long ago its associations were dark and mysterious. Many illegal executions took place here, away from the prying eyes of the law, and it was a popular place for duels to be fought, as well as secret romantic meetings. In its time it was also a haunt for Ladies of the Night (it is known that Robert Louis Stevenson had a great interest in the evening trade on Calton Hill). Today the hill is a veritable mausoleum of monuments and had Edinburgh's best architects tried to conceive a suitable building for these pieces, they could not have come up with a more perfect setting than the one nature has provided.

Arthur's Seat
HOLYROOD PARK

Arthur's Seat is Edinburgh's most famous natural landmark. Rising dramatically to 251 metres (823 ft) above sea level, this impressive volcanic crag gives off an air of ancient calm. It has seen the area's first people settle at its foot; it has seen the building of the castle on the rock to the west and the growth of the city around it; it has stood silent sentry while battles raged below, and the history of a nation unfolded.

It is believed its name derives from the ancient Gaelic phrase 'Ard-na-Said', or 'Height of Arrows', a reference either to its previous use as an old hunting ground, or to its lofty position. Arthur's Seat is reached by a roadway that starts in Holyrood Park, and it is well worth the climb. From the summit of the crag a panorama of a typical Scottish landscape can be seen – truly one of the finest in the Lothians. On a clear day, it is even possible to see the southernmost peaks of the Highlands. It is a local tradition to greet the summer solstice from the top of Arthur's Seat and, despite the crowds, is one of this beautiful city's loveliest customs.

The Pentland Hills
SOUTH-WEST EDINBURGH

It has been said that the Pentland Hills are a miniature version of the Highlands, and they are just as beautiful, if slightly less dramatic. They run south-westwards from Edinburgh in a rolling green stretch nearly 8 km (5 miles) wide.

The village of Swanston (see page 180) is nestled at the foot of the Pentlands. The writer Robert Louis Stevenson spent some time here, and he is said to have had a great love of the area, particularly the hills surrounding the village. This is perfect walking country, and there are a number of routes that can be followed through the hills. It is even possible to follow the old paths made by the cattle drovers in centuries past. All the walks provide an abundance of spectacular views, and the landscape is truly magical. Higher up in the hills, the moorland is carpeted with heather and bracken, and small streams and rivers wend their way through the high grasses. This is one of the best places to escape to from the bustle and noise of the city centre.

Bass Rock
FIRTH OF FORTH

The strange lump of basalt known as 'Bass Rock' lies 2½ km (1½ miles) out in the Firth of Forth, and for centuries has been a landmark for sailors, because of the lighthouse that stands on it, and because of its distinctive size and shape. Bass Rock, another of Edinburgh's volcanic legacies, is 1 mile in circumference and 107 metres (350 ft) high.

This rock has been made use of over the years – from early times a castle stood here, evidence of which can still be seen. It is also said that the seventh-century hermit St Baldred made his home on Bass Rock and later died here. The young James I stopped on the rock on his way to seek sanctuary in France in 1406. Both Covenanters and Jacobite rebels have been imprisoned on the rock.

Today, like many other islands in the Forth, Bass Rock is a harsh and uninhabited place, haunted by seabirds, particularly gannets, whose cries echo through this relic of Scotland's history.

Fireworks
THE OLD TOWN

For three weeks in August each year, during the Edinburgh International Festival, the city comes alive with drama and spectacle, culminating in the Military Tattoo on the castle esplanade. Breathtaking firework displays, such as the one pictured here, have become a common feature. Full of pomp and circumstance against the magnificent backdrop of the floodlit castle, they light up the impressive Edinburgh skyline for miles around, a fitting end to the celebrations.

It is not only at Festival time that the city plays host to such displays, though. All year round, Edinburgh is haven of lively activity and entertainment. Street performers and bagpipers can be found on every corner and in every open area across the city; the theatres, of which Edinburgh has an abundance, provide a surprising variety of shows, from West End musicals to the very latest in alternative drama. Opera, comedy, film, professional and amateur alike, are all catered for here. It cannot be denied that Edinburgh is the social and cultural heart of Scotland.

Statues in Waverley Market
PRINCES STREET

The Waverley Shopping Centre is one of Edinburgh's most successful modern developments. Situated in the heart of the city's commercial area, at the east end of Princes Street, the underground centre is much admired for its tasteful interior design, replete with plants and water.

Its roof serves as a popular stage for street performers, a wide open piazza made of pale grey granite – a striking contrast to the honey-coloured sandstone that characterises the majority of the New Town. The curious collection of statues that adorn this roof-top enhance the modern feel of the area. They were created by the English sculptor Crispin Guest and erected in 1991. As the sun rises in the east these eerie figures are silhouetted against the backdrop of Princes Street and the nearby Waverley Station, creating a dramatic spectacle. Despite the predominance of classical statues and monuments all around Edinburgh, there are a also number of modern sculptures like these to be found, indicating the old city's willingness to embrace the new.

Clock Tower
PRINCES STREET

The clock tower at the east end of Princes Street is one of the most dramatic and dominant features of Edinburgh's impressive evening skyline. As night falls over the New Town, an astonishing array of illuminations – on shops, monuments, public buildings and especially the North Bridge – set the whole area aglow with their light and colour. The richness of many of the old buildings is shown off to its best advantage by this modern enhancement.

The clock tower is actually part of the Balmoral Hotel, situated near Waverley Station, and it is the *pièce de résistance* of this magnificent building: it stands 59 metres (192 ft) high on the top of a bold, square tower. The clock's face is floodlit at night and can be seen for many miles around. Surmounting the clock itself is a wrought-iron lantern. For many years it has been a tradition to keep the clock running two minutes fast, so that travellers using Waverley Station will be in time for their trains.

Fidra Lighthouse
FIDRA ISLAND

This lighthouse stands on Fidra Island, one of four small islands off the coast of North Berwick. The other three islands are Craigleith, Lamb and Eyebroughty. Robert Louis Stevenson spent a few years of his childhood here, and it is said that Fidra was the early inspiration for his best-loved novel *Treasure Island*. Despite his later travels across the world, eventually making his home in Samoa, Stevenson was to remain profoundly affected by the people and the places he experienced during his youth in Scotland. Fidra is now a wild and forlorn-looking place, rocky and dark – a perfect place to let the imagination run wild. As well as the lighthouse, Fidra is home to the ruins of an ancient Celtic monastery, some of the oldest such remains in the Edinburgh area.

This photograph was taken from the shores of Yellowcraig, a beautiful, sandy, dune-scattered beach surrounded by picturesque woodland, wild grasses and flowers. Stevenson also spent much time here in his youth, and Yellowcraig's influence can also be seen in his novel.

Poppy Fields
DUNBAR

Poppy fields are frequently associated with battle sites, and these fields, a short distance from the town of Dunbar, are no exception. Dunbar has been the site of some of the most notorious battles in Scotland's history. In 1295 the Battle of Dunbar saw Edward I of England defeat the Scots. This disastrous turn of events eventually led to the English seizing Edinburgh Castle – an advantage they retained for some years. Some centuries later Oliver Cromwell and his army of Roundheads beat the supporters of Charles II in a decisive battle near Dunbar, that claimed the lives of 3,000 Cavaliers.

Dunbar has two main features that have enhanced its strategic importance throughout the centuries: its harbour and its castle. The harbour saved Edward II from certain death as he made his escape from here after the Scots' victory at the famous Battle of Bannockburn. Mary, Queen of Scots was brought to Dunbar Castle after her abduction by Bothwell, and later they sought sanctuary here during the turmoil that preceded Mary's downfall in 1567. The castle was destroyed by Mary's half-brother shortly afterwards, but this emotive ruin still echoes with the voices of Scotland's past.

TRADITION & ENTERTAINMENT

From its plethora of theatres, hosting every conceivable entertainment, through traditions such as the One O'Clock Gun, to the spectacle of the famous International Festival, Edinburgh is a city whose vitality is evident at every turn.

Ghost Tours
THE OLD TOWN

Edinburgh's history abounds with tales of mystery and murder. The ghosts of tormented souls walk the streets and closes of the Old Town relentlessly – or so Edinburgh locals would like to make one believe. Although many of these chilling tales are likely to be the result of generations of vivid imaginations, there are also many that are indeed true: the history of Deacon Brodie (the real Dr Jekyll and Mr Hyde), Burke and Hare (Grassmarket's notorious murderers and body snatchers) and many other Edinburgh citizens are rooted in fact.

The ghost tours are some of Edinburgh's most popular tourist attractions, and despite their obvious commercialism, should not be missed. A costumed guide will walk you round the streets of the city, telling tales of bloody executions, murderous revenge, ghosts, ghouls and witches. There are a number of different tours to choose from, ranging from the light-hearted to the truly spine-chilling, but most end up in the recently discovered vaults beneath the Old Town and the cold, damp and dark caverns heighten the atmosphere of mystery and horror.

Ross Open Air Theatre
PRINCES STREET GARDENS

In the summer months, one of the main attractions in the Princes Street Gardens is the Ross Theatre. This huge open-air venue, often sheltered by a vast canopy, provides many distractions and a whole series of varied events. It is especially popular with children, for whom talent contests and other targeted entertainments are provided. But it is a place for all the family, and other shows such as traditional Scottish dancing draw crowds every day, with people hovering around the edges, participating as much or as little as they like. The informal atmosphere it encourages is one of its greatest attractions.

Its other great asset, though, is its situation: the Gardens lie just to the east of the flamboyant Ross fountain, under the watchful eye of the castle, and all around, the verdant lawns and bright colours of the Gardens stretch out to form a peaceful and beautiful cultivated landscape.

Edinburgh Festival Fringe

Although the original Festival was intended to be essentially an operatic event, it excited the interest of a number of theatre groups, which turned up in 1947 and played out their performances wherever they could find the space and the audience. This sowed the seeds of what was to become the Festival Fringe.

The Fringe was officially established in 1951, and had a small party of organisers independent of the Festival proper. It has always encouraged a wide variety of performers and maintains a broad-minded attitude to the definition of entertainment. As a result, the Fringe has incorporated eclectic artistic styles and abilities right from its outset. It has proved to be the launch pad to the big-time for many individuals and shows.

Although they are two separate events, the International and Fringe Festivals have become mutually dependent. Together they provide the widest variety of entertainment found in any one city. Numerous other festivals have grown up around them and now Edinburgh in summer provides something for everyone; all tastes, ages and nationalities.

Edinburgh International Festival

Established in 1947, in an effort to relieve the darkness of the post-war era, the Edinburgh International Festival found so much success that its lavishness, experimentalism and world-wide renown has grown every year since.

The original concept was based around a massive operatic gathering, organised by Rudolf Bing, administrator for the Glyndebourne Opera. For the first few years of the Festival, opera was its main focus. Eventually, the spectrum of entertainment broadened to encompass almost every genre imaginable: dance, theatre, musical, ballet, comedy. Classical and contemporary, amateur and professional, the good, the bad and the downright bizarre were all welcomed.

Today, thousands of people from all over the world flock to Edinburgh in August and September to witness this spectacular event. Every conceivable space is turned into a stage for all manner of performances. Parties, parades, the traditional and the unexpected all meet on the streets of Scotland's capital to make up what is now the largest festival of arts in the world.

Military Tattoo
EDINBURGH CASTLE

For all the hundreds of different entertainments to come out of the Edinburgh International Festival, there is one that has become a major focal point and the single most enduring and popular event to take place at this time – the Military Tattoo.

Since the Festival began in 1947, thousands of people have taken their places on summer evenings on high-rising scaffolding seats constructed either side of the Castle Esplanade to watch perhaps the world's most famous military tattoo. The Scottish regiments, all in full military uniform and regaled by the inescapably Scottish music of the pipes and drums, perform precision marches and military movements and recreate historical events. The show is gloriously Scottish – although regiments from all over the world frequently guest in the Tattoo – overpoweringly emotive and, climaxing with fireworks and a lone piper playing the Last Post from the ramparts of the floodlit castle, it is one of the highlights of the Festival calendar, and a true celebration of Scottish history and tradition.

Scots Guard
EDINBURGH CASTLE

The Scottish Division of the British Army is made up of seven regiments, and each of these has played its own part in Scotland's glorious military history. Born of war-like peoples, the Scots have an unprecedented reputation for courage and military prowess. This is more than likely due to the continued attacks from their marauding southern enemy, as Scottish history from the earliest times will testify.

Edinburgh's main regiment is the Royal Scots, or the Royal Regiment. It is the oldest of the seven Scottish regiments, and was founded in 1633 by Sir John Hepburn, while attempting to raise an army to fight under Louis XIII of France. The new group of men he gathered together distinguished themselves in this service amongst the ancient French regiments. A member of the Picardy Regiment, no doubt somewhat slighted by the achievements of the Scots, boasted that the Picardys had been on duty the night of Christ's Crucifixion, drawing the famous retort from the Royal Scots' colonel: 'if we had been on guard, we should not have slept at our posts' – earning the Scots the nickname 'Pontius Pilate's Bodyguard'.

Guards like this can be seen in and around the castle, which, even today, works as a military operation.

Traverse Theatre
CAMBRIDGE STREET

As one would expect from the city that spawned the Festival Fringe, Edinburgh has, particularly in recent years, become one of the leading lights in experimental drama. The free-for-all nature of the Fringe means that anyone with any inclination to perform is able to do so, and this has uncovered some major talents on the alternative scene.

The Traverse Theatre is the focal point in Edinburgh for this genre. The theatre was first built in the early 1960s in an effort to maintain a year-round interest in the avant-garde, rather than just having a burst of fascinated enthusiasm for three weeks of the year. The original theatre was housed in St James's Court and could house only 60 spectators, and by 1969 was forced to set up anew in the Grassmarket. Here, it slowly gathered a good reputation and in 1991 it moved to its new, prestigious home in Cambridge Street. A far cry from its humble origins, the new theatre was purpose-built with a magnificent auditorium and stage, all reflecting the unusual nature of its repertoire. The theatre continues to draw the crowds, all coming to witness new, unusual and often *risqué* drama in surroundings that mirror the theatre's success.

Festival Theatre
NICOLSON STREET

The dramatic glass-fronted Festival Theatre seems strikingly out of place amongst the typical grey and sandstone buildings on the south side of the city, near the University Old Quad.

It began its life in 1892 as the Empire Theatre, burning down less than 20 years later, and it stayed a shell for some time. Reconstruction work was completed in 1928 and for a while the theatre regained its former popularity. Eventually this began to wane and by the 1960s, its use as a home for the performing arts had been usurped by the somewhat less glamorous role of a bingo hall.

The magnificent modern structure standing here today is the result of a major redevelopment programme, completed just a few years ago, which aimed to restore the theatre to its former glory. Elements of the original Empire Theatre have been retained within the building, while other parts have been extended and modified to such an extent that the Festival is now the main home to opera in Edinburgh. The programme is not exclusive though, and a variety of performing arts can be enjoyed here. It is a part of Edinburgh's cultural history that has fortunately not been abandoned.

Usher Hall
LOTHIAN ROAD

The eye-catching structure of Usher Hall has a curiously contradictory air of old-fashioned opulence and timeless modernity. Its octagonal exterior is enhanced by columns and canopies, archways and stone carvings. Inside, the semi-circular auditorium is crowned with a domed copper roof and sprinkled with just enough gilding to lend it a sense of luxury, but not so much that it becomes overwhelming.

All in all, the Hall is an appropriately elegant building, drawing crowds of music and opera lovers every season. Constructed just before the outbreak of the First World War, the money for the Hall was bequeathed by one Andrew Usher – a strange legacy for a local brewer.

Like the many other purpose-built venues in Edinburgh, Usher Hall becomes the epicentre of musical life during the Festival, but it hardly lies dormant during the rest of the year. Throughout the winter, the Hall plays host to the Scottish National Orchestra, and a variety of musical extravaganzas can be seen here all year round.

Royal Highland Show
INGLISTON

Ingliston, situated near Edinburgh airport, is just a short drive out of the city centre. It is here that one of the area's best-loved annual events takes place – the Royal Highland Show. The show invades the area every June and provides a great family day out, with many different attractions, exhibitions and 'hands on' experiences.

Epitomising Scottish agricultural life from past to present, the fair hosts shows of the famous Highland cattle, sheepdog trials and show-jumping. There are demonstrations of forestry techniques and farming methods, but most spectacular are the motorcycle display teams and parachute jumps.

The Scottish Agricultural Museum, which can be visited all year round, has many different exhibitions explaining the rural way of life, the hardships and rewards, machinery and methods of Scottish agriculture. During the Highland Show, further exhibitions complete the picture of how people lived off the land in times past.

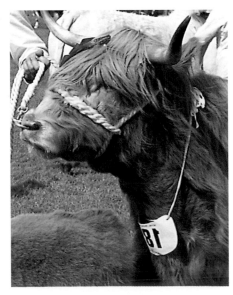

Edinburgh Zoo
COSTORPHINE HILL

No city's attractions are complete without a zoo, and Edinburgh boasts one of the finest. Spreading over 80 acres across Costorphine Hill on the outskirts of the city, the whole complex commands fine views of the city and surrounding countryside.

Opened just prior to the outbreak of the First World War, Edinburgh Zoo was remarkably modern in its design and planning. The animals are housed comfortably in spacious enclosures, and every effort has been made to recreate as natural an environment as possible for them.

Although the zoo has over 1,000 different species within its confines, it is best known for its penguins. Four different types are kept here, with nearly 200 altogether. Every day there is the famous 'Penguin Parade' through the zoo – a great tourist attraction, and immensely popular with children. Another of Edinburgh Zoo's magnificent sites is its free-flying Night Herons, which can be seen in the evenings, sweeping by overhead.

One O'Clock Gun
EDINBURGH CASTLE

This tradition is now so much a part of everyday life in Edinburgh that the residents of the city hardly hear the noise of the gun, let alone pay it any heed. The gun is situated on Mill's Mount Battery, one of the castle's loftiest sites, whose vantage points offered great protection and opportunities for defence in the city's turbulent past. For most of the day, the battery is simply one of the best places in the city to view the spectacular surroundings, which encompass Arthur's Seat and the Firth of Forth, but every day, except Sunday, crowds gather at the appointed hour to watch this old Edinburgh ritual being executed.

The tradition dates back to the days when ships sailing in and out of the Forth used the signal to check their chronometers. At exactly the same moment as the gun is fired, a time ball drops in the Nelson Monument on Calton Hill, at the east end of Princes Street. This too was a signal to sailors, and the accuracy of these two events occurring simultaneously every day was, in its day, considered to be a miracle of modern technology.

Procession
ROYAL MILE

For a long time after the construction of the New Town – and indeed for a while before – the Old Town was a place of dirt and slums, of poverty and disease, and the contrast between the two parts of the city was acute. It was only in the nineteenth century that efforts were made to clean up the Old Town, making it desirable and habitable once again. For a long time the rich tapestry of history that makes up the Royal Mile and the surrounding area was forgotten.

Today, of course, the historical sights in the Old Town are Edinburgh's main attraction, but a sense of competition between the old and the new still hovers in the air. The Old Town Renewal Trust organises a number of events every year that prove that, although the south side of the city may be old, it is still alive and kicking. These include numerous processions up and down the Royal Mile, such as the one pictured here, which are nomally accompanied by drums and bagpipes, celebrating the Old Town's history. There is also 'Doors Open Day' every September when the many attractions along the Royal Mile – from the Outlook Tower to the plethora of museums – open their doors to the public free of charge.

Playhouse Theatre
GREENHOUSE PLACE

Perhaps in no city in Britain other than London is there such a concentration of theatres and entertainment venues as Edinburgh. But this is only to be expected from a city that every year hosts the largest festival of arts in the world. Like the International Festival in August, the city's theatres provide entertainment and attractions to suit every age and every taste – all year round.

The Playhouse Theatre is Edinburgh's answer to London's West End. It is a large venue, with an auditorium that can seat 3,000 people. The theatre suffered great damage in a fire in the early 1990s, but it has been carefully restored and is now bigger and better than ever. It is here that the most popular musicals play when touring, and the neon lights often advertise successful shows from the West End or Broadway. But the Playhouse is not reserved exclusively for musicals. It is the local indoor venue for pop concerts – even opera has been performed here. It gives the impression largely of being a young person's theatre though, even showing films occasionally. It is only during the Festival that the Playhouse gives itself up to more classical productions, when it plays host to large-scale ballet.

Museum of Childhood
HIGH STREET

It is a well-known irony that the Museum of Childhood was founded by a with a notorious dislike of children. Town Councillor Patrick Murray set up the museum from his own collection of toys and games, intending it to be seen as a social study rather than, as its name implies, a museum geared specifically towards children.

Five storeys, packed with childhood memorabilia, have a universal appeal for both old and young. The museum was the first of its type, and the founder's original collection has been much enhanced by gifts from all over the world, from people who liked the idea of a museum dedicated solely to such exhibits. Everything can be found here; from toys made of wood, metal and every other conceivable material to Britain's largest collection of dolls. Timeless classics like the train set are displayed alongside toys and games that have been the subject of brief but all-consuming trends over the past decades.

Children will love it and parents will sigh over it, but will also hopefully appreciate Murray's sardonic humour which permeates much of the museum, most obviously in the appropriately inappropriate window at the museum's entrance – a memorial to King Herod!

ARCHIBALD·CAMPBELL·MARQVESS·OF·ARGYLL
BEHEADED · NEAR · THIS · CATHEDRAL · A·D·1661
LEADER·IN·COVNCIL·AND·IN·FIELD·FOR·THE·REFORMED·RELIGION
"I set the Crown on the King's Head
He hastens me to a better
Crown than his own"
BANK HOTEL
ST. MARGARETS CHAPEL

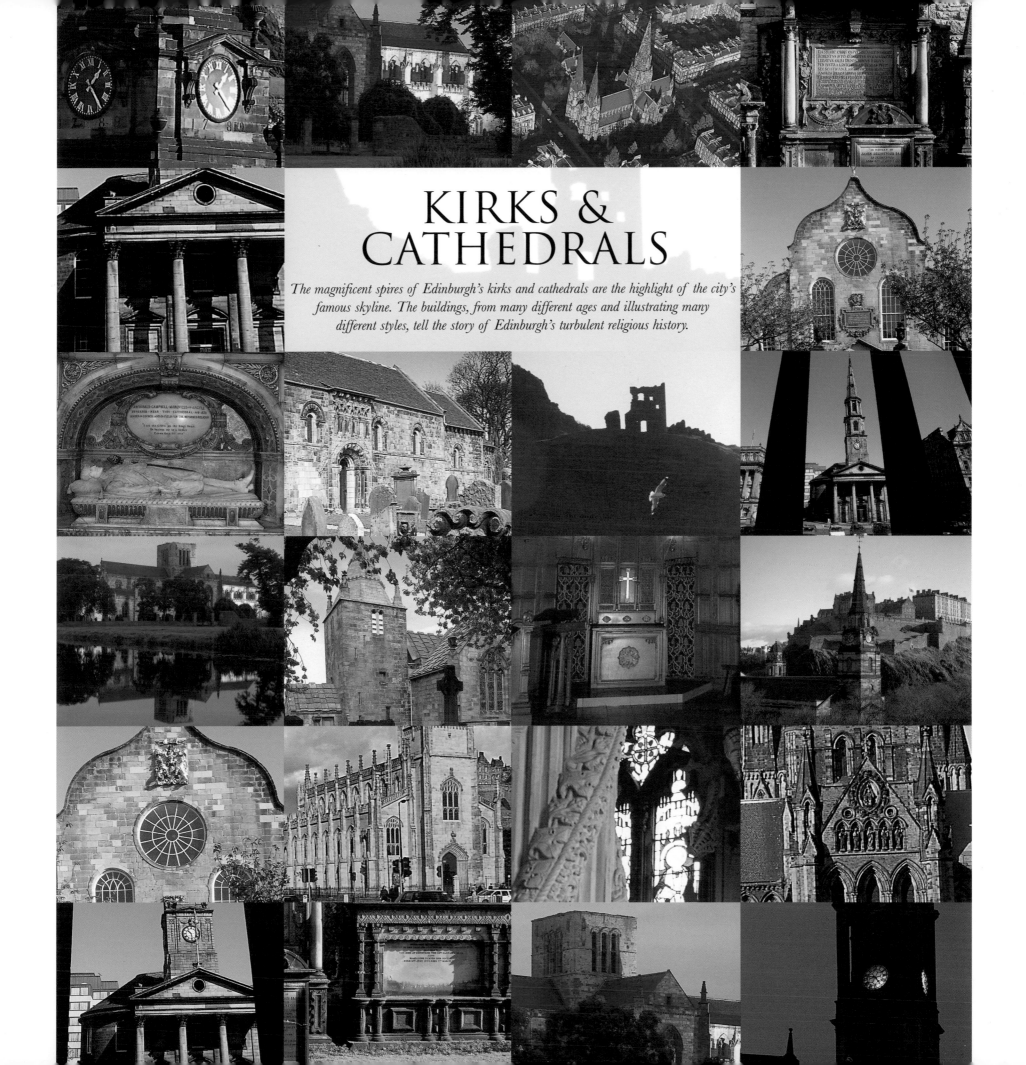

KIRKS & CATHEDRALS

The magnificent spires of Edinburgh's kirks and cathedrals are the highlight of the city's famous skyline. The buildings, from many different ages and illustrating many different styles, tell the story of Edinburgh's turbulent religious history.

St Mary's Episcopalian Cathedral
PALMERSTON PLACE

The great entrance doors to St Mary's are embellished with fine ironwork, above which are carvings of Christ, John the Baptist and the Apostles. Walking around the outside of the building, one can only marvel at the skill with which these and the many other carvings have been executed – all around the gables and even high up on the triple spires, figures of various saints have been lovingly worked.

The interior of St Mary's has a lot to live up to and, although the magnificence of its outward appearance is not quite matched by its inner designs, it is none the less an impressive and atmospheric place: long aisles covered by grand, medieval-style interlinking arches stretch the length of the nave and unusual diagonally placed buttresses, centring on four main pillars, support the lofty height of the main spire.

In the north transept, near the pulpit, is the chapel dedicated to Charles I (Charles the Martyr), who founded the Edinburgh Episcopal Church in 1633. He was executed in 1649 and the chapel contains depictions of the king holding a crown of thorns, the symbol of his martyrdom.

Aerial View
St Mary's Episcopalian Cathedral
PALMERSTON PLACE

This photograph gives some idea of the immensity and grandeur of St Mary's Episcopalian Cathedral. Its main spire is one of the most instantly recognisable features of the Edinburgh skyline, and the cathedral building itself dominates the west end of the New Town. St Mary's is the largest church to have been built in Scotland after the Reformation.

Its relentlessly Gothic exterior belies its actual construction date of 1879, with the west tower and the twin spires dating from the early twentieth century. That the cathedral's dark and intricate appearance seems authentic is a tribute to its designer, Sir George Gilbert Scott. The funds to build such a magnificent cathedral came from Barbara and Mary Walker, whose initial plan was to commission a simple chapel dedicated to the memory of their mother. At the time, there was no Episcopalian cathedral in the diocese. St Giles – a short distance from the castle, on the Royal Mile – briefly enjoyed the status of cathedral twice during the seventeenth century, after which it was handed back to the Presbyterians and became a High Kirk once more. Thus, the projected chapel never materialised, and the architectural enormity that is St Mary's was born.

St John's Kirk
LOTHIAN ROAD

Standing unassumingly at the end of Princes Street, St John's Kirk is surrounded by the hub of Edinburgh's busy main shopping precinct andcan easily be overlooked. It is worth taking the time to investigate the church, though, as well as wandering through its overgrown yard.

Dating from the early nineteenth century, the design of St John's consists of just a nave and aisles, with no transepts. The eight bays that divide the nave are ornate with pinnacles and buttresses, and carvings of biblical figures abound in the shafts. There is a sense of harmony about the whole building, inside and out; even the chapel and vestry, both of which were added in the twentieth century, are absorbed easily into the whole.

Around the sides and back of the church, away from the busy street corners, gravestones and monuments lie in abundance on and around the small crumbling walls and overgrown pathways. From here, the sheer wall of St Cuthbert's Kirk blocks the view to the south and the visitor is tempted over the walls by the intriguing wilderness of neglected graves beyond.

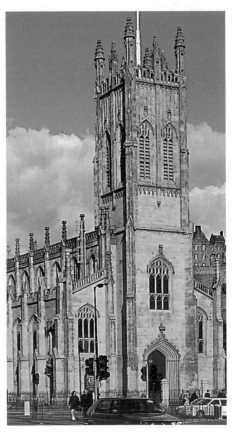

Dalmeny Kirk
DALMENY

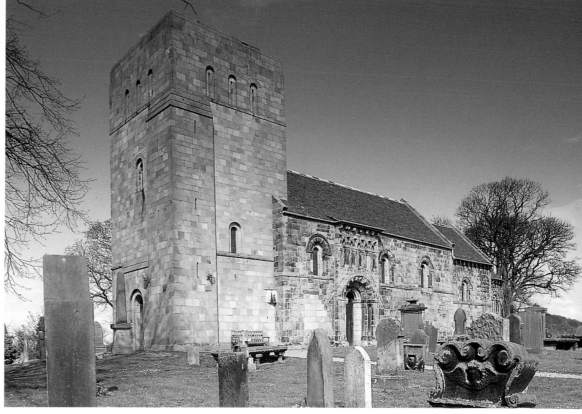

It is difficult to believe that Dalmeny Kirk actually dates from the twelfth century, so unaffected by time and progress does it appear. In almost every way, it is the finest example of its kind to be found in Scotland. Its perfectly ordered, complete exterior is enhanced by magnificent stonework and Romanesque carvings. These carvings are remarkable, but the strange figures of beasts adorning the south doorway, despite having endured nearly 800 years of wind and weather, are particularly notable.

The satisfaction gained from wandering around the kirk's exterior and ancient kirkyard is maintained inside. Its simple form is not marred by over-decoration – for example, the vaulting is confined to the small chancel and apse, with none to be found in the nave.

The quality of this kirk, its exquisitely preserved aspect and its situation as the focal point of the beautiful village of Dalmeny make this a fascinating and thought-provoking historical place.

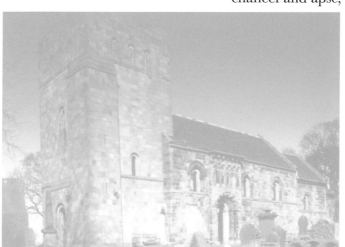

St Mary's Church
HADDINGTON

The church of St Mary's in Haddington was completed in the mid-1400s, but it was to survive only a hundred years before invading English armies wreaked havoc on it, leaving it a roofless shell. Although some restoration work was done on the nave shortly afterwards, large parts were left to crumble and decay. Surprisingly, this large and beautiful building was left this way for four centuries, until the decision was made in the 1970s to restore the church to its former glory.

How glorious it now is. Its size is its most impressive feature; large, but not imposing. Inside, it is airy and spacious, bathed in a glow from the stained-glass windows, which include one by the Pre-Raphaelite Edward Burne-Jones. Some of its other fascinating features are the 'Green Men'. These peculiar mythological creatures are carved in the fine stone, and depict strange human figures with foliage sprouting from their mouths, representing the association between man and nature. Green Men are quite common in Scottish churches and cathedrals, and those here at St Mary's are fine examples.

St Andrew and St George's
GEORGE STREET

When the plans for the New Town were drawn up, they included the two main squares, St Andrew's and Charlotte, each one with its own church. However, the site of the church in St Andrew's Square was quickly bought by Sir Laurence Dundas, who proceeded to build his own mansion house there – now the Royal Bank of Scotland headquarters (see page 76) – thus forcing the Town's planners to find a new site for their church. They settled upon the east end of George Street, and what is now known as the church of St Andrew and St George's was built.

This was the first of the New Town's many churches, designed by Major Andrew Frazer of the Royal Engineers and opened for worship in 1784. Best known for being the setting for the Great Disruption in 1843, when hundreds of clergy left to form the Free Church of Scotland, St Andrew and St George's has an unusual appearance. The theme of its oval exterior is continued inside, with a curving gallery and a rounded ceiling. Its simplicity is refreshing amongst the predominance of Gothic architecture that characterises much of Edinburgh.

Tron Kirk
HIGH STREET

Christ's Church at the Tron was built to take the influx of people from St Giles when it underwent one of its brief periods as an Episcopalian Cathedral in the mid-seventeenth century. Lacking in ornamentation, and some would say beauty, the Tron Kirk is still a fascinating reminder of Scottish religious and civic history.

Its original plan was T-shaped, but the south side was destroyed when the road bisecting the Royal Mile from the North Bridge was built in the 1780s. Half a century later, a fire further rendered the building's original shape unrecognisable and destroyed the old wood and iron tower and steeple.

It has not been used as a kirk since the 1950s and now houses the Old Town Information Centre: a humble end for such an historic place. Recent excavations have changed the focus of the building, and a visit here still brings surprises, for within the kirk walls, under its still-fine hammerbeam roof, one of Edinburgh's oldest roads, Marlin's Wynd, has been uncovered. This paved pathway is believed to have been named after Walter Merlion, the man responsible for first paving the Royal Mile in the sixteenth century. The archaeological look of the ground, enclosed in the severe kirk building, with its stained-glass windows still intact, provides a fascinating and unusual scene.

St Margaret's Chapel
EDINBURGH CASTLE

Although it is named after St Margaret, wife of King Malcolm, the first monarch to build a residence on Castle Rock, the chapel was actually built in the century after her death in 1093, perhaps by her son King David I. It is now the oldest surviving part of the castle, and throughout the centuries the chapel has seen many uses, most degradingly as a storeroom for gunpowder – its original purpose was at first neglected, then eventually forgotten, and it was not until the mid-1800s that its medieval role as a chapel was re-discovered and restoration work began.

It is not altogether surprising that the chapel's importance was over-looked for centuries, for it is a small, unadorned, rectangular building, no more than 9.1 metres (30 ft) long, with only five small windows. Today these windows are one of the chapel's focal points: the beautiful, brightly coloured stained glass standing out in the simple interior. Each window depicts an illustrious Scottish character or saint: William Wallace, St Andrew, St Columba, St Ninian and St Margaret herself. The windows are twentieth-century additions, but somehow enhance the religious and medieval atmosphere of the chapel.

Canongate Kirk
CANONGATE

It is quite possible to overlook the small Canongate Kirk, down towards the end of the Royal Mile. The whitewashed building, set back from the road and hidden behind a cluster of cherry trees, is as far removed in appearance from almost every other house of religion in Edinburgh as it could be.

Its origins lie with the nearby Holyrood Abbey. The Abbey served for many years as the parish church of the Canongate but, in 1687, King James II ordered that the chapel there be turned over for the use of the Knights of the Order of the Thistle. The new church was designed by James Smith (who was a Roman Catholic like the king – an unusual state of affairs amidst the warring Protestant factions of seventeenth-century Edinburgh – a fact which led to the monarch's deposition shortly after this time and which probably explains the anomaly of the kirk's cruciform structure).

Further surprises await inside the kirk, which is bright and spacious. Natural light floods through the clear glass windows – no stained glass here – illuminating the simple nave and aisles. Understated it may appear, but both the history and unexpected appearance of the Canongate Kirk make it worth a stop on the way to Holyrood.

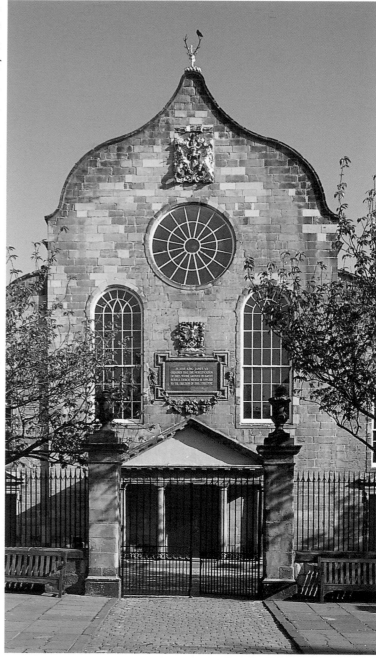

Apprentice Pillar
ROSSLYN CHAPEL

Seven miles away from Edinburgh, on the outskirts of the Esk Valley, lies one of the most magical places in Scotland – Rosslyn Chapel. Built in the mid-1400s by William St Clair, this extraordinary place has the most marvellous collection of religious carving and sculpture anywhere in Britain.

It is this, the Apprentice Pillar, that is the finest and the most famous piece in the building. Encircled at the base by a series of winged serpents, four leafed vines climb from the bottom in a majestic swirl. The story surrounding this is a popular local legend. It is said that a master mason and his apprentice were working on the chapel, when the mason was called away. On his return he saw that the apprentice had carved this pillar and, in a fit of rage and jealousy, killed the boy. Elsewhere in the chapel, figures of the mason and his apprentice (depicted with a head wound) can be found. This is no more than a romantic tale, and nobody really knows the reason why Rosslyn Chapel is home to so much craftsmanship, but this only adds to its mystique.

St Anthony's Chapel
HOLYROOD PARK

High on a rocky crag in Holyrood Park sit the ancient ruins of St Anthony's Chapel. The chapel is a forlorn and mysterious site. No one has ever established exactly why, or for whom, the chapel was built on this isolated spot. It stands as the only mark of human life in this area, and there is no evidence of any other building or habitation around it.

What is known is that this building dates from the fifteenth century and was once made up of the small vaulted chapel with a room situated on the west side, presumably the priest's sleeping quarters.

A number of explanations for the chapel have been suggested. The most commonly accepted is that it was in some way associated with a hospital that had been established at Leith, which specialised in the care of people suffering from 'St Anthony's fire', a form of eye disease. The genuine purpose of this small chapel will probably never be confirmed, but it is a curious feature in this most spectacular landscape.

St Cuthbert's Kirk
LOTHIAN ROAD

The kirk that stands here now is mainly a late nineteenth-century reconstruction, but this relatively modern structure hides a long history. It is believed that St Margaret founded a church here in 1127, which altered gradually over the centuries until by the mid-seventeenth century it was a long, narrow building with just a tower and a south transept. The changes continued and evidence suggests that by the eighteenth century St Cuthbert's consisted of an eclectic mixture of buildings, a tower and the ruins of the older versions of the church.

It is not surprising then, that the present church has an odd, unidentifiable quality about it – a quality, it should be said, that givees it an added aspect of intrigue. From the outside, a visitor would not expect much from the interior of St Cuthbert's, but this is where the real pleasure of this kirk lies. Inside, wide, spacious transepts are offset by marvellous Corinthian pillars, intricately carved stalls and a beautiful mosaic floor.

The rambling graveyard is another of St Cuthbert's curiosities; Alexander Nasmyth is buried here along with hundreds of others, whose memorials make for a fascinating afternoon's wandering.

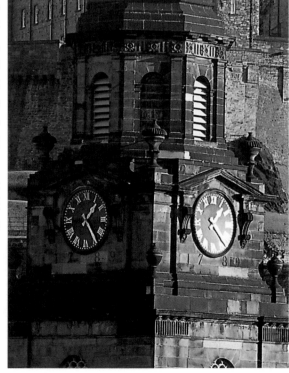

Costorphine Church
COSTORPHINE

Costorphine manages to retain a medieval sense of peace and solitude despite its proximity to the city centre, a reflection of the ancient rural parish it once was. Like many old churches, Costorphine has been extended and rebuilt over the centuries so that today it is a curious mixture of architectural styles, and echoes the religious history of a number of different eras. Medieval in origin, a chapel was built next to the church at the turn of the fifteenth century, to which a chancel and a tower were added a few years later. Further renovations took place in the mid-1600s when the chapel had a porch added and the church itself was razed and rebuilt. Most of the present church is the result of further rebuilding in 1828, when the chapel was finally absorbed into the church building.

Despite its many changes, the medieval character of the church is predominant, even in the interior – a careful nineteenth-century renovation. The tombs set into recesses along the inside are particularly fine and include those of Sir Adam Forrester, the man responsible for building the original chapel, and his wife.

Greyfriars Kirkyard
GREYFRIARS

The historic Greyfriars Kirkyard sadly spends much time swamped with tourists, all clamouring to see the grave of the famous 'Greyfriars Bobby' (see page 132). But if you are fortunate enough to visit it at a quiet time, the impression it makes is truly breathtaking. The small but attractive kirk stands in the centre of the kirkyard and all around it grassy lawns spread out, with a small scattering of free-standing headstones; crooked, mossy and picturesque. Impressive funerary monuments and wall memorials cover every inch of the crumbling stone walls around the edge, the majority blackened and worn with age. The grandiose vaults are decaying and broken, but their magnificence is not diminished, for their essence remains. The list of people buried here is distinguished: the poet Allan Ramsay; James Craig, the man whose vision shaped the New Town; and the architect family the Adams, whose marble-carved vault stands out bright amidst the grey of the other monuments.

Here, in 1638, the National Covenant was signed – the beginning of the long struggle between the Scottish Presbyterians and the Episcopalians, followers of the new religion established by Charles I. Here, some 40 years later, over 1,000 Covenanters were imprisoned. An iron gate separates this prison from the kirkyard, and nearby the Martyr's Monument pays homage to all those who died in this fight for religious freedom.

High Kirk of St Giles
HIGH STREET

The High Kirk of St Giles has been the religious heart of the Old Town for centuries, and is now a majestic and impressive reminder of Edinburgh's turbulent religious history.

A church has stood on this spot since 854 AD, gradually being rebuilt and extended. Named after the Patron Saint of Cripples (a popular saint in medieval times!), the Norman kirk which replaced the original was destroyed in 1385 by the English. A Gothic replacement was built during the fifteenth century, and the church became once again the focal point of Old Edinburgh. It was not to last long – as the tide of the Reformation swept the country, St Giles suffered the loss of some of its finest fixtures and fittings.

The honorary title of 'Cathedral' is really a misnomer: it was officially a cathedral only twice, only then for brief periods. The first time was in 1633, when Charles I established Episcopacy in Scotland, and then later in the century during the Covenanters' Rebellion. Episcopacy was eventually abandoned and St Giles reverted to its old title of High Kirk.

The interior is breathtaking. Aisles – including this, the Argyll aisle – altars and chapels lie under the light of the rich stained-glass windows, which date from various periods, from Pre-Raphaelite to the modern west window commemorating Robbie Burns.

Thistle Chapel
High Kirk of St Giles
HIGH STREET

The Thistle Chapel is a relatively modern addition to this old kirk. Built between 1909 and 1911 by Sir Robert Lorimer, the chapel is dedicated to the Knights of the Order of the Thistle, one of the oldest chivalric orders in Scotland. The Order of the Thistle was established in 1687 by James VII, and since that time has consisted of a small group – the monarch and 16 others. The Knights of the Thistle still attend a special service annually in the chapel.

It is a tiny but breathtaking corner of the kirk. Extravagantly (some have said over-indulgently) carved, every inch of the chapel is a testimony to the workmanship of William and Alexander Clow, the two Edinburgh men responsible for the fantastic detail. The chapel was carefully designed to reflect the fifteenth-century origins of the present kirk, and the bossed roof, granite floor, ribbed vault and elaborate stalls successfully blend in with the Gothic style of the rest. The effect is overwhelmingly opulent and it is worth taking some time to sit and appreciate the handiwork, and to try to find the wee oak-carved angel playing bagpipes amongst the myriad of carvings.

LIFE & CULTURE

Modern life in Edinburgh has grown up from the city's cultural roots, and the old and the new survive harmoniously together, from the beautiful architecture of old to the very latest in sports stadiums and business centres.

Scotch Whisky Heritage Centre
CASTLEHILL

The production of whisky is one of the oldest industries in Scotland and it is a symbol that is inextricably linked with the country.

The Scotch Whisky Heritage Centre, just down the Royal Mile from the Castle, is one of the Old Town's premier tourist attractions, but while it is undoubtedly a highly commercial enterprise, it also offers a fascinating insight into Scotland's best-known export. Exhibitions illustrate the history of the product, complete with sights, sounds and smells from the various ages. The distilling process is explained, and the different whisky-producing regions and types of whisky are discussed. It charts the progress of the whisky industry, from its origins to its present-day success. Samples of the different whiskies are available to try, and for those with a taste for the liquor, just about every variety imaginable can be bought here.

Royal Museum of Scotland
CHAMBERS STREET

The building housing the Royal Museum of Scotland was designed by a captain of the Royal Engineers, Francis Fowke, in the mid-1800s. It is a large, low, quite imposing building, constructed from pink sandstone. The central block of the museum is only two storeys high, although the wings have three levels. The only obvious external ornamentations are the urns and balustrades adorning the façade over the entrance.

The interior is marvellously spacious, most obvious in the Great Hall, a magnificent and unusual room – all glass and cast iron – with a high ceiling supported by elegant iron columns. The inspiration for this design came from London's Crystal Palace, and it gives the whole museum a sense of modernity that is quite at odds with some of its collections.

The eclectic mixture of exhibits found here include art and sculpture, relics of ancient civilisations from around the world, dinosaurs, evidence of ancient industrial practices ... the list is endless: there is something here to please all visitors.

Parliament Square
HIGH STREET

Parliament Square, despite its name, is now the legal heart of the Old Town. Surrounding the High Kirk of St Giles, this area was once occupied by the kirkyard. Parliament House was built in the seventeenth century, but the frontage seen today is the result of later additions made to designs by Robert Reid in the early nineteenth century.

Parliament House was used as the seat of the Scottish Parliament until the Act of Union in 1707, after which it was rendered obsolete. Its purpose then changed and it became the Law Courts (Scotland's legal system remained independent from England's, even after the Union) and the Supreme Court of Scotland still holds session here. Today the two great attractions within Parliament Square are the Great Hall of Parliament House, which boasts a fine hammerbeam roof, and the extravagant Signet Library, designed by William Stark.

Waverley Station
PRINCES STREET

When the proposal to run a railway through Princes Street Gardens was first made in the 1830s, it was vehemently opposed by the residents. As Princes Street became less residential and more commercial, however, resistance lessened. This was, after all, the age of industry and Edinburgh, as Scotland's capital, felt the pressures of progress. In 1846, the railway was constructed.

The fact that the Gardens remain as beautiful today as they were when first laid out, is testament to the care and consideration that was made in the planning and building of this railway. By creating tunnels and building embankments, the railway was hardly noticeable. It did not – and still does not – encroach upon the beauty of this area.

Two stations sprang up, built by rival rail companies, Princes Street to the east and Waverley to the west. With these came the first two major building developments on the south side of the street: the great railway hotels, the Caledonian and the North British (now the Balmoral – see page 83). Today, just as in the nineteenth century, these two magnificent buildings serve the customers of the rail lines, and along with the station itself, they are fitting testimonies to the industrial age.

Old Observatory
CALTON HILL

The two observatories on Calton Hill were built within 30 years of each other. The first, pictured here, is the Old Observatory and was designed by the architect of the New Town, James Craig. This round-towered, three-storeyed building was the brainchild of a Leith man who was inspired by the marvel of a telescope owned by his brother, an optician. He decided to build an observatory that people could come and pay to use. Work began on the building in 1776, but the design was extravagant and ambitious and funds were slow to come in. Consequently, the observatory was not finished until 1792, by which time the impetus had waned somewhat, and it was never the success that the businessman envisaged.

The City Observatory is another of Calton Hill's testimonies to William Playfair, who built it for his uncle, an astronomer, in 1818. This observatory is open to the public, and is also host to the Edinburgh Astronomical Society. These were both eventually overtaken in popularity by the construction of the Royal Observatory at Blackford Hill, but their ideal hilltop situation ensures a continued interest in both their style and purpose.

Camera Obscura
CASTLEHILL

The building that now houses the camera obscura was once a tenement housing block, built in the seventeenth century. In 1853, its height was utilised by the installation of the camera obscura and since then has drawn thousands of visitors each year who come to marvel at this piece of nineteenth-century technology.

The original camera obscura was installed by Edinburgh optician, Maria Theresa Short, but this was replaced by Patrick Geddes' instrument when he bought the building in 1892. The device is situated in the building's distinctive black and white dome and is a marvellous cinematic extravaganza. A system of lenses and mirrors revolve to produce a telescopic view of the city that is projected on to a large, white table. Here one can watch everyday life going on below, as well as appreciate close-ups of the architecture of nearby buildings.

The building also houses a number of related exhibitions, including International Holography and Victorian Edinburgh, and makes for a fascinating journey through the city, past and present.

The City Chambers
HIGH STREET

The buildings that now house the City Chambers were designed by John Adam as a Royal Exchange. This was part of an attempt by the city council in the late eighteenth century to encourage the local merchants and traders to move their business from the streets into open offices. However, it soon became clear the merchants preferred to ply their various trades on the streets and, loath to see the building go to waste, the city council moved their head offices here.

The appearance of the Chambers is delightfully deceptive, for from the front the buildings appear to be only three storeys high. Built right on the ridge of the Old Town, however, the sheer drop is accommodated by up to 12 storeys at the back.

Beneath the foundations of the City Chambers lies Mary King's Close. This was one of the first places to experience the Plague when it reached the capital in 1645 and, in an attempt to contain the disease, the whole close was sealed off and the people left to die. Mary King's Close was eventually opened again, and the bodies cleared away, but the whole area was later completely covered by the City Chambers. It is said that the ghosts of those who died in the close still haunt this part of the Old Town.

Register House
PRINCES STREET

Walking north across the bridge from the Old Town brings you to one of Edinburgh's most stately buildings – Register House. Situated at the north-east corner of Princes Street, this was built from designs by Robert Adam in the 1770s, specifically to house Scotland's historical records. It has continued to serve this purpose ever since; the first place to be custom-built as a record office.

The building's exterior is not overly ornamented, featuring just a pedimented centrepiece and four columns. Extensions to the building were made in the 1830s, but fortunately these were to the rear of the building, so its smooth, neo-classical façade was not destroyed. It is simple, elegant and appropriately distinguished. Its interior is magnificent, the main feature being the domed ceiling, complete with detailed plasterwork and gilding.

Register House is open to the public, who can investigate the thousands of fascinating records here. Although certain collections of records have, by necessity, been housed elsewhere, this remains one of the most important, and beautiful, of Edinburgh's public buildings.

Edinburgh International Conference Centre
MORRISON STREET

As well as being a popular holiday destination, Edinburgh has also become one of Scotland's main thriving business centres. In order to cater for the ever-growing commercial and business side of the country's capital, a number of modern structures have been built, and today Edinburgh can keep up with the greatest European cities, boasting facilities of all kinds. It is an essential part of Edinburgh's modern culture and lifestyle.

Work began on the Edinburgh International Conference Centre in the early 1990s and it opened in 1995. Somehow the modern building does not look out of place in a city characterised by sixteenth-, seventeenth- and eighteenth-century structures; a testimony to the skill of its architects. Equipped with all the latest facilities, the Conference Centre has a unique, multi-purpose auditorium, that unusually, can be divided up into three separate auditoria, or used as one main one, which can seat up to 1,200 people.

Royal Bank of Scotland
ST ANDREW'S SQUARE

St Andrew's Square is now the financial heart of the city of Edinburgh, and many of the palatial former residences have been transformed into offices and company headquarters. While the outward appearance of the square has not changed much since it was built in the eighteenth century, the activity going on within the walls of the stately Georgian houses is very different.

The building housing the Royal Bank of Scotland headquarters is one of the most beautiful in the square. The site on which it stands was where Craig originally envisaged St Andrew's Church, but before these plans could get off the ground, the land was bought and developed by Sir Laurence Dundas. He commissioned Sir William Chambers to design him a suitable town house and the result was this marvellous mansion, completed in 1774.

After Sir Laurence's death, the building was acquired by the Excise offices and later, in 1825, by the Bank of Scotland. Much of the inside has been changed to accommodate its new purpose, but the main hall in particular, a mid-nineteenth-century addition characterised by star-shaped windows, makes a visit to the bank an unusual experience.

West Register House
CHARLOTTE SQUARE

The building that now houses a large part of the Scottish Record Office was once St George's Church. James Craig had planned to have a church in each of his two squares, Charlotte and St Andrew's, but his plans were foiled before they could get off the ground and St Andrew's Church had to be built instead in George Street (see page 52). Charlotte Square got its church, however, built by Robert Reid in 1824. The cost of realising Robert Adam's lavish designs proved prohibitive, and in the end the church only vaguely resembled them. The result is a noble but simple affair, with just four columns rather than Adam's original eight and no extraneous ornamentation. The dome remains one of the dominant features of Edinburgh's skyline, reaching a height of 46 metres (150 ft).

In the 1960s, the interior of the church was renovated to make way for the Public Record Office, and today it houses hundreds of government records, as well as a fascinating exhibition on Scottish history. The building has, since its construction, been the focal point of Charlotte Square, and it continues to be so, despite its change of use.

National Gallery of Scotland
PRINCES STREET

The National Gallery of Scotland is one of the finest pieces of architecture to grace the Princes Street area, and is a suitably sumptuous building for the fine works housed within it.

The Gallery was designed by William Playfair, whose original plans actually included a number of grand features which never made it off the drawing board, due to a restriction of funds. This, however, does not detract from the magnificence of the stately columned porticoes and the graceful exterior.

Inside, the design is as carefully planned as the outside. Two galleries are divided into ten octagonal rooms and later additions include an upper floor containing a further five galleries, and a basement that was cleverly built to provide more space within the Gallery without spoiling Playfair's marvellous exterior.

The National Gallery houses the finest collection of painting and sculpture to be found anywhere in Scotland. The exhibits include pieces from all ages, and works by numerous renowned international artists: Raphael, Van Dycke, Rembrandt, several of the Impressionists, as well as many by English and Scottish painters. The collections of work by Edinburgh's own Sir Henry Raeburn are the pride of the Gallery.

Divinity College
EDINBURGH UNIVERSITY

The foundations of the University of Edinburgh were set in the late sixteenth century. In 1580, Clement Little, a local man, donated his vast collection of books to the city in order to found a library, and from this grew the Town College, which received its Royal Charter in 1582 from King James VI.

The oldest surviving part of the University, and still the very soul of the establishment, is the Old Quad. This was designed largely by Robert Adam, but was built after his death, and the influence of William Playfair, who modified Adam's designs, can also be felt. The Old Quad was completed in 1789, and consisted of just one of Adam's projected quadrangles, as well as the spectacular Upper Library.

The University campus now spreads over a wide area in the city, and the Old College is no longer the central seat of learning. It is, however, the finest of all the university buildings. Over the years some of Britain's most brilliant scholars have passed through the University's gates, especially those in the field of medicine, in which Edinburgh has a world-wide reputation for excellence.

Murrayfield Stadium
WEST EDINBURGH

Edinburgh caters for sporting fanatics of all kinds, and sports stadia, grounds and courses can be found both in and around the city centre. The best-known and all-encompassing is the Meadowbank Stadium, situated near the breathtaking landscape of Holyrood Park. Smaller venues, pools, tennis courts and a plethora of other sites make indulging in a sporting life very easy in Scotland's capital.

To the west of the city lies the Murrayfield Stadium. This is the home of Scottish international rugby, and throughout the season it hosts Scotland's home games against the best in the sport. As is befitting an international sporting arena, Murrayfield is a fine modern stadium, and has recently been renovated to keep in line with the very latest in the sport's developments. It attracts thousands of rugby fans every year to watch the games – both international and domestic.

Meadowbank Stadium
NEAR HOLYROOD PARK

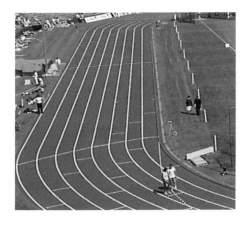

Meadowbank is Edinburgh's foremost sports stadium and the biggest arena in the city for sporting events of all kinds. Over 80 sports are hosted here throughout the year at both international and domestic levels.

The stadium is situated to the north-east of the striking landscape of Holyrood Park and caters for both indoor and outdoor activities. It has a huge, modern athletics track and a velodrome; inside all manner of sports can be indulged in, including the latest sporting trends such as rock-climbing.

Meadowbank was built in 1970 when Edinburgh was the host city for the Commonwealth Games. Its most impressive achievement is the stadium itself, in which 15,000 spectators can be seated around the track under its enormous cantilever roof. It was clearly a success as the Commonwealth Games returned to Meadowbank in 1986, placing Edinburgh amongst Europe's leading sporting cities.

Braid Hill Golf Course
BRAID HILLS

The natural plateau on the top of the Braid Hills made this the ideal place to build a golf course, but the topographical suitability was only one of the factors that encouraged golfing fanatics; the exceptional views from the Braids make this the perfect setting for a day's golfing. The City of Edinburgh acquired this land towards the end of the nineteenth century, and there are now two full courses here in the Braids, both publicly owned and offering more than just the opportunity for a little relaxation. Golfing is a popular pastime in Scotland, no doubt largely due to the great number of picturesque spots and open spaces throughout the country. There are six municipal courses in the Edinburgh area alone, but none could have a more stunning location than the Braid Hills.

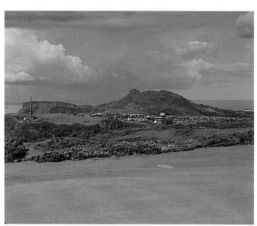

At an elevation of 206 metres (675 ft), the views from the Braids are unsurpassed. The visual spectacle must be a distraction even to the most dedicated of players, with the Firth of Forth stretching out to the horizon and the ancient wooded valleys of the Braid Burns spreading out mysteriously below.

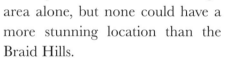

Balmoral Hotel
PRINCES STREET

One of the most exclusive hotels in Edinburgh, the Balmoral is honoured to be one of the few constructions allowed on the south side of Princes Street, after an Act of Parliament forever preserved the Gardens and views of the Old Town. The rise of this awe-inspiring building came at the same time as the rise of the railway in the city. It was one of two grand hotels built by the companies that owned the railways in the early twentieth century. The other, the Caledonian, stands at the west end of the Gardens.

The Balmoral was originally named the Great British, but this was changed when objections were voiced (North Britain being another – not well-liked – name for Scotland). It is a massive square building, made from the same golden sandstone that is so popularly evident throughout Edinburgh. The hotel is highly ornamented, boasting bow and dormer windows, false balconies and a clock tower. It has recently been renovated and is now a high-class establishment with all the modern conveniences.

THE OLD &
THE NEW

From the crowded closes of the Royal Mile, through the splendid baronial tenement estates to the sweeping avenues of the Georgian New Town, each part of Edinburgh carries haunting echoes of the ages through which it developed.

THE ROYA

CASTLEH

The New Town
NORTH EDINBURGH

The development to the north of the Old Town could not be more different from the ancient part of the city. Beautifully designed residences line the straight, symmetrical streets, and everything fits into a careful plan: churches, houses, public buildings and avenues all complement one another. Some say it lacks the dynamic spirit of the Old Town, but the New Town has a character all of its own: stately, regal and unassumingly opulent.

The two men responsible for the success of the New Town were: George Drummond, Lord Provost, whose imagination and determination it was to develop a new town on the edge of the old one; and James Craig,

the chief architect, whose genius is evident in so much of the work. Craig's grid of streets and squares was organised around the main thoroughfare, George Street, with two squares, St Andrew's and George Square (later renamed Charlotte Square) on either side. Running parallel to George Street were two subsidiary streets, Princes Street and Queen Street. Little did Craig guess that it would be Princes Street, not George Street, that would eventually become the heart of the New Town. Work began on the New Town in 1767, after permission to extend the boundaries was finally granted, and the magnificent Georgian sweep of the town slowly began to take shape.

The Old Town
SOUTH EDINBURGH

The Old Town grew up around the rocky crag on which the castle sits, and by the eleventh century a track had been forged between the castle and Holyrood Abbey below: the beginnings of what is now known as the Royal Mile, the spine of the Old Town. Leading from this, many side streets – or wynds – and closes developed, and it is this intriguing network of ancient streets that characterise this part of the city. Although many disappeared beneath later developments, particularly during the nineteenth-century slum clearances, this street pattern is still very much in evidence.

It was neither a healthy nor particularly pleasant place in which to live: from medieval times people lived close together – packed into the high buildings – and disease spread easily. By the mid-1800s, an estimated 40,000 citizens lived in this small area. It was this overcrowding that finally sent people across the bridge to the north, where the New Town offered more spacious and less dangerous habitation. The exodus was large-scale though, and the Old Town suffered greatly as a result, the population eventually sinking to below 3,000. Recent restorations have ensured that the Old Town is now enjoying a revived popularity, without losing any of the mystique that gives it its character.

VICTORIA STREET
THE OLD TOWN

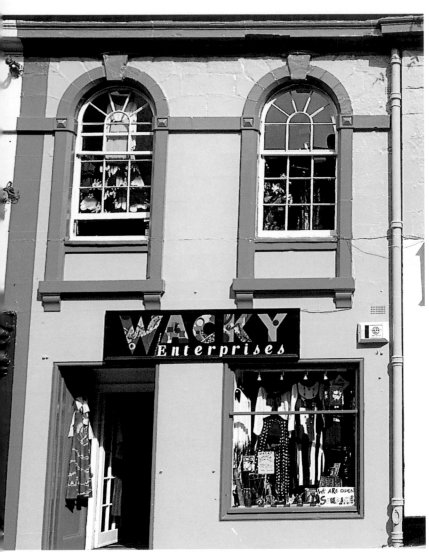

To the south of the Royal Mile, Victoria Street, part of an area formerly known as West Bow, rises up to George IV Bridge. Set back from the overcrowded closes of the Royal Mile this was one of the most desirable and fashionable places to live in the eighteenth century, helped by the founding of the first Assembly Rooms here in 1710. A few of these residences still stand on the north side of Victoria Street.

Towards the end of the century this part of the city, like much of the rest of the Old Town, began to experience a decline, and for 50 years the street deteriorated. Developments in the early part of the nineteenth century, which included the construction of George IV Bridge, saw a new rise in fortunes for Victoria Street, although many of the old buildings were pulled down in the name of progress.

Today, Victoria Street boasts an interesting medley of period houses and arcaded shops and, although it has not quite recaptured the vitality of its heyday, it makes for a captivating stroll through this part of town.

White Horse Close
CANONGATE

At the bottom of the Royal Mile, near the iron gates of Holyrood Palace, is one of the most picturesque of all Edinburgh's closes. Whitehorse Close was once of prime importance to travellers to and from Scotland's capital: it was here that the long and arduous journey to London by stage-coach began. The old coaching inn here is believed to be where Charles Edward Stuart's officers lodged in 1745, before the army embarked on their march to London.

The oldest buildings in the close date back to the early seventeenth century, but renovations and restorations over the years mean that many of them have been lost. The quaint whitewashed exteriors that characterise the close today set this apart from the dark and somewhat cramped closes further west. The typical Scots architecture is inescapable though, and the two-tiered houses with their gables and outside stairways add to the feeling of harmony and order that pervades the close.

Moray Place
THE NEW TOWN

When the New Town was completed in the nineteenth century, development of the north side of Edinburgh continued, until a third age of construction was accomplished. This became known as the Second New Town, spreading north and westwards.

Moray Place is one of the finest examples of the architectural style that characterises the newest phase. Designed by James Gillespie Graham, it was built on land owned by the Earl of Moray. Moray wanted the estates on his land to be completely different from the symmetrical, straight streets of Craig's plan, and so Graham devised an unusual series of streets, crescents and circuses. Moray Place is the pinnacle of his achievement. It is a massive, 12-sided block of high buildings, each one four storeys. Situated evenly around the perimeter of the circus are columned centrepieces and pilasters, enhancing the sense of upper-class luxury that pervades this area. So successful was the design that the Earl of Moray himself actually moved into this street (number 28).

St Andrew's Square
THE NEW TOWN

This was the first part of the New Town to be built – with the corresponding Charlotte Square on the other side of George Street. Unlike Charlotte Square, however, this has a fascinating mixture of architecture. Over two centuries, new and contrasting buildings have sprung up in St Andrew's Square, each one representing its own style and era. As well as the original Georgian houses that line the north side, there are structures from all ages, most notably the Guardian Royal Exchange building, a curiously individual black and white structure, erected in the 1930s.

The square is dominated by the statue which stands in the fenced-off central green. Commonly known as the 'Melville Monument' this is a memorial to Henry Dundas, the first Viscount Melville. A key political figure in the government of Pitt the Younger, it is now known that Melville's methods were somewhat dubious, but he none the less held great sway over the constituencies in Scotland in his time. The extent of his power is borne out in his nickname, 'Harry IX, uncrowned king of Scotland'.

Castlehill
THE ROYAL MILE

The beginning of the Royal Mile is the narrow street known as Castlehill which stretches from the castle Esplanade to where the road widens into the High Street. A plethora of buildings relate the history of this area, many of them to the castle itself.

Among the best-known buildings on Castlehill is the seventeenth-century Cannonball House. This is named after the cannonball that is lodged in the gables. Opinion is divided on exactly how it got there: local tales would have us believe it was fired from one of the great guns on the Mills Mount Battery during Bonnie Prince Charlie's brief occupation. The less romantic say it was put there in the nineteenth century in an effort to attract tourism. Either way, it is a talking point.

From Castlehill, cobbled steps lead down to the Grassmarket (see page 166), one of Edinburgh's most notorious places and the site of execution, murder and subterfuge. Other buildings of interest along this stretch include the Outlook Tower and Tolbooth St Johns, whose spire forms an unmistakable part of the Edinburgh skyline.

The Mound
THE NEW TOWN

The unromantically named Mound came into being shortly after construction of the New Town began. Before the boggy Nor' Loch was drained, there was no convenient way of travelling between the New Town and the Old. This became a problem for those who lived in the Old Town, but saw the opportunity for business in the New.

Such a man was George Boyd, an Old Town tailor who, with the rise in popularity of the north of the city, found trade somewhat scuppered by the lack of a direct route. He began to form a makeshift walkway with planks and stones that ran from the Lawnmarket on the Old Town ridge down to the eastern end of Princes Street. The idea caught on, and soon many people were contributing to 'Geordie Boyd's Mud Brig'. The excess of earth and mud that came about from the building of the New Town soon ensured that a permanent track was established here. In its early days it must have been an unattractive sight across the valley; time and landscaping have now turned it into one of Edinburgh's most picturesque roads.

North Bridge
THE NEW TOWN

When the plans for the New Town were accepted in the 1760s and the possibility of the city being extended to the north became a reality, it was realised instantly that the first step in this new plan was to build a bridge connecting the two parts of the city. Many metres below the Old Town ridge lay the marshy and unattractive Nor' Loch, creating a natural barrier between south and north. Almost immediately, work began on draining the loch and the first North Bridge was completed in 1772. The sturdy, three-arched structure was the first milestone in Edinburgh's New Town development.

The bridge that now spans the valley was built in the 1890s, an enforced reconstruction due to the arrival of the railway in Edinburgh, and it is a marvellous sight. It carries the road from the Royal Mile at the Tron Kirk over Waverley Station and the Princes Street Gardens to the thoroughfare at the east end. It is worth pausing to appreciate the vista from the bridge: to the east lies the sweep of Arthur's Seat and the Salisbury Crags, and to the west stretches Princes Street Gardens and the spires and buildings of the New Town.

Tenement Housing
MARCHMONT

The word 'tenement' tends to conjure up images of council estates and crumbling, closely packed buildings, but no vision could be more out of place with regard to Edinburgh's tenements. There is little sign of poverty here, and today estates like Marchmont are inhabited largely by the city's middle classes.

The first appealing feature of Marchmont is that it lies on the edge of the parkland commonly called the Meadows, wide open spaces of green lawns and woodland. But it is not only its situation that makes it a desirable habitat. The fine Baronial architecture is one of its main selling points, and the tenements are as rich in their own way as any of the marvellous Georgian buildings in the New Town.

The estate was built on land owned by Sir George Warrender, who saw a lucrative business opportunity in developing this land into housing estates. By the late 1860s, plans were on paper and construction was ready to begin. The rich architecture is largely thanks to Warrender's determination that sub-standard and ugly buildings would not grace his land. A network of extravagant Scottish Baronial structures arose, and Edinburgh's middle classes flocked to rent their properties, having found a more suitable niche than the overwhelming and expensive New Town or the slums of the Old.

Fan Window
THE NEW TOWN

A walk across the North Bridge from the Old Town to the New is like travelling to another city completely. In style, atmosphere, attitude and history, these two parts of Edinburgh could not be more different.

The most immediately noticeable, and striking, difference is the architecture. The Old Town is characterised by mysterious wynds and steep alleyways lined with high tenements and densely packed, ancient-looking grey buildings – every house seems huddled over its own closely guarded secrets. The New Town, in total contrast, is bright, open, neat and majestic. It was laid out in a grid-like network of streets and connecting avenues, and all the buildings had to conform to a standard of design and construction to keep the aesthetic whole harmonious. The golden sand-stone buildings are enhanced by classical ornamentation: Corinthian pillars, carved panels, balustrades and pediments abound. Georgian windows and fanlights are found everywhere, adding to the orderly and unified aspect of the whole New Town. The finest works of some of Scotland's greatest architects and designers can be found here, including members of the Adam family, Sir William Chambers and James Craig, the father of the New Town.

The Royal Mile
THE OLD TOWN

Roughly following the ridge of the Old Town, the Royal Mile extends from the foot of the castle to the Palace of Holyroodhouse below. It is divided into four sections: Castlehill, the Lawnmarket, the High Street and Canongate, each with its own objects of interest and particular tales to tell.

Shops, historical buildings and museums combine in a fascinating mixture of the old and the new. To either side of the street, numerous closes and wynds offer an insight into Edinburgh's past. The Royal Mile has a dark and enclosed feeling, due to the great height of many of the buildings. This feature dates from when the city was surrounded by fortified walls and houses had to be built high so as to accommodate the huge population living within such a small area. This adds to the brooding atmosphere of mystery that abounds here, and as one walks down the street, through the ancient market places, past the place of public execution, past the Old Tolbooth that was once the prison, enjoying the varied churches and ancient winding alleyways, it is impossible not to feel awed by the history echoing from every step.

Princes Street
THE NEW TOWN

Now the busiest street in Edinburgh, Princes Street was originally a subsidiary road in the plans for the New Town. However, when the railway was built in the nineteenth century, Princes Street became an important thoroughfare and it has risen in prominence since then.

Lined on the north side by rows of shops, it is the south side that offers the most interest. Flanked by the magnificent Princes Street Gardens, dotted with memorials and statues, including the Scott Monument, and boasting some of the finest architecture in the city in the form of the galleries, the Balmoral Hotel and others, a walk along here is truly a journey of discovery. An Act of Parliament has forbidden any further development on this side of the street, so that the vast ridge of the Old Town, with the crag and the castle, will always be seen unobstructed, a reminder of Edinburgh's ancient past from the centre of its modern life.

Mylne's Court
LAWNMARKET

This is one of the oldest closes that remains in Edinburgh's Old Town, a large number having been destroyed during the large-scale clearance projects that helped rid the city of many of its slum areas, while causing numerous fine old buildings to be irretrievably lost. Mylne's Court dates from the late seventeenth century, and is named in honour of Robert Mylne, one of Edinburgh's pre-eminent architects and Charles II's master mason, who had a hand in the current design of the Palace of Holyroodhouse at the opposite end of the Royal Mile.

Only two of the tenements that Mylne designed are still standing and these have been converted into student houses (perhaps nowhere else in Britain do students have the honour of residing in such historical surroundings!). Despite this, they give a clear idea of how the whole close must once have looked. Rising to seven storeys, including an attic, the buildings have quite an austere appearance, but in their day were considered quite stately, and there is nowhere better to gain an idea of how life must have been lived in the seventeenth- and eighteenth-century Old Town.

Charlotte Square
THE NEW TOWN

Charlotte Square is the epitome of the New Town, its reality as perfect as its concept. One of two grand squares (the other being St Andrew's, see page 91) that were designed to flank the main thoroughfare of George Street, the plans for Charlotte Square were drawn up by Robert Adam. Although the initial design, consisting of classical palace façades, embellished by carved panels and balustrades never came to fruition, Adam's influence still pervades the glory of the square.

The north side is the closest example of Adam's vision for the square: 11 houses around a central section, characterised by eight large pillars and guarded at either end by stone sphinxes. These are not the only unusual ornamental features to be found here: amongst the fine architecture lurk stone-hewn Grecian urns, carved pediments and many other embellishments. To see the interiors of these houses, one must visit the National Trust-owned 'Georgian House', at number 7. This gives a good idea of the lifestyle and trends of upper-class culture in the eighteenth century.

Ramsay Garden
CASTLEHILL

Ramsay Garden was named after the poet Allan Ramsay who lived here in the mid-1700s in the octagonal 'Goose-Pie House'. A building of his own conception, the house has a view down to the foot of the Mound, where the poet's statue stands on the edge of Princes Street Gardens. This strange building is characteristic of Ramsay Garden's peculiar aspect, but despite this, it was this particular development that began the Old Town's revival.

The man responsible for this revival was town planner Patrick Geddes, who bought some land here towards the end of the nineteenth century and immediately set about constructing blocks of flats whose character made up for what they lacked in uniform design. In complete contrast to almost anything else in Edinburgh, the flats in Ramsay Garden were half-timbered with picturesque red roofs and a quaint, rambling character. They were an immediate success, drawing the more affluent members of Edinburgh society back into the arms of the Old Town. They are still some of the most desirable residences in the area.

Ann Street

STOCKBRIDGE

Ann Street is the most beautiful road in Stockbridge, and the pride of the suburb. Its design is attributed to the architect James Mylne, and it is both unusual and strikingly quaint.

The houses which rise up on both sides of Ann Street are at first hidden from view behind rows of trees and lilac bushes, and are set back, each with its own carefully planted and maintained gardens at the front. Further investigation, however, reveals rows of magnificent palace fronts, enhanced by pediments and pilasters, columns and balconies in a staged effect, each row set a little back from the others, and each row of varying heights. This abundance of classical architecture in the middle of this quiet, garden street is astonishing, and the architect would have been pleased with the effect that Ann Street still has on visitors. No detail has been left undone, and the overall effect is completed by iron railings and ornamental lamps. It is a truly exquisite achievement.

103

PARKS & WATERS

In the heart of Edinburgh's busy centre, landscaped lawns provide a tranquil respite, and on the outskirts of the city, placid stretches of water – rivers, canals, lochs and harbours – add a shimmering grace to the countryside.

Princes Street Gardens
PRINCES STREET

Where the beautifully land-scaped Princes Street Gardens now lie was once a bog, the Nor' Loch, which stretched across the valley from the rocky ridge of the Old Town to the north. The loch was drained in 1759 and the residents of Princes Street planned and planted the Gardens, reserving them for their own private use. By 1816, it was decided that the south side of the street be kept free from all further development, preserving the beauty of this open space. This agreement has largely been kept to, despite the proximity of the railway, and in the 1870s the Gardens became common ground, open to the public.

Today the park is divided into two parts: the West and East Gardens. These are separated by the National Gallery and the Royal Scottish Academy on the Mound. Within, the Gardens are not only large stretches of bordered grass, but also pathways that lead to smaller areas, such as the Heather Garden and the Peace Garden. Here is an escape from the frenetic activity of Princes Street and an atmosphere of calm and solitude.

The Floral Clock
PRINCES STREET GARDENS

Princes Street Gardens are full of pleasant surprises: statues, monuments and memorials are artlessly scattered amongst the carefully land-scaped and lovingly tended parkland, and pathways lead to unexpected areas of enclosed tranquillity. One of the most unexpected features of the Gardens, however, is the Floral Clock.

Hidden just below the street where the West Gardens descend from the Gallery entrance and at the foot of the statue of poet Allan Ramsay, one of Edinburgh's most famous citizens, this working clock is constructed entirely from plants and flowers. It is fascinating to stand and watch the huge minute hand move around, and wait for the announcement of the hour, which comes from a wooden cuckoo in a wooden bird house to the left of the clock.

Planted in 1903, the Floral Clock is believed to be the oldest in the world, but it does not look its age. Each year, it is planted with new flowers, and in the summer, its vivid colours and unusual character draw hundreds of people, locals and tourists alike, to admire this marvellous piece of horticulture.

Dunsapie Loch
HOLYROOD PARK

Like St Margaret's Loch, also situated in the park, this is a man-made stretch of water, intended to enhance the park. This it certainly does, and is a popular attraction for tourists, who picnic before starting the ascent to Arthur's Seat which rises dramatically behind it. This is the easiest point from which to start the climb, which is 137 metres (450 ft) above the loch, ascending by way of the road that winds its way to the top.

The loch itself is 122 metres (400 ft) above sea level and commands magnificent views across the diverse park landscape and surrounding area. Many wild birds have made their homes here, including ducks and swans. The small island in the middle of the loch was created especially to provide a nesting place for these birds, encouraging them to stay, and they seem undisturbed by the constant toing and froing of human visitors.

Fishmarket
NEWHAVEN

The seafaring tradition that is still so evident in Newhaven began in the fifteenth century when James IV decided that this was the place to build his warship, the *Great Michael*. Legend has it that the ship needed all the trees in Fife to build, but it was never used: perhaps this is why Newhaven never really took off as a shipbuilding port. Instead, it turned its attentions to the fishing trade, and for many centuries the wealth of the village depended on the catches of herring and oysters that were to be found in the Firth of Forth.

By the nineteenth century, Newhaven oysters were famous world-wide and a huge oyster fishery thrived here. Sadly, the interference of the English again put the mockers on Scottish progress, this time not in the form of marauding armies, but by one George Clark, who leased the fishery, overshipped the area and left Newhaven all but bereft of its livelihood. Today, only echoes of the eminent fishing port that Newhaven once was remain. The lively fishmarket has gone and pleasure boats rather than fishing boats sit in the harbour. Newhaven's fortunes have been somewhat revived recently, with the establishment of Harry Ramsden's restaurant in what was the old fishmarket, and the port still offers a fascinating insight into the old seafaring traditions.

Sunset
THE FIRTH OF FORTH

Yonder the shores of Fife you saw;
Here Preston-Bay And Berwick Law;
And, broad between them rolled,
The gallant Firth the eye might note,
Whose islands on its bosom float,
Like emeralds in gold.

Sir Walter Scott

The Firth of Forth is the main natural landmark in the Edinburgh district. It is a magnificent stretch of water, and picturesque villages that once drew their living from it lie along its shores. Small harbours are remnants of once-thriving fishing and trading communities. More dramatically, the coastline is scattered with the haunting ruins of medieval castles and stately homes. The Forth Islands are largely uninhabited now, and play home to scores of wild birds and water creatures, such as otters and even the occasional seal. Fishing is a popular pastime in the Forth waters and tributaries, where trout and salmon can be found.

From the high points of Edinburgh, from the castle ramparts, from the top of Calton Hill and Arthur's Seat, the Forth can be seen stretching out, magical and shimmering, part of the life and culture of the city since earliest times.

Royal Botanic Garden
INVERLEITH

Just north of the New Town lies yet another surprisingly tranquil area of parkland – the Royal Botanic Garden. This rich and splendid garden was not always situated here, though, and as one of the oldest botanic gardens in Britain it has a long and fascinating history.

Its origins lie with the University, when one of the Royal College of Physicians' founders began a small physic garden near Holyrood. The interest this generated forced it to move to an area near what is now Princes Street and a few years later, it moved again to Leith Walk. Each time, the Garden grew in magnificence, encompassing a wider variety of plants and flowers than the medicinal herbs it originally grew.

Finally, in 1823, the Garden moved to its present site in Inverleith. It now stretches over 70 acres and includes areas of finely landscaped lawns and picturesque woodland. It is also home to some of the best collections of unusual and exotic plants to be found anywhere in the country. Most spectacular are the rhododendrons, which are a breathtaking site in the spring months, and these alone make the garden well worth a visit.

The Glasshouse
Royal Botanic Garden
INVERLEITH

In the heart of the Royal Botanic Garden stands a collection of variously aged greenhouses, known as the 'Glasshouse Experience'. These are home to fantastic collections of exotic plants and are one of the Garden's greatest assets.

There are 11 plant houses altogether, ranging from the Victorian Palm House to the New Glass Houses, built in the 1960s. The glasshouses alone are a point of interest, their differing architectural styles each a reflection of the age in which they were designed: the Palm House, built in 1858, is a medley of cast-iron columns and stairways, appropriately decorated; the New Glass Houses built on frames of tubular steel with modern elevated walkways and suspension cables.

Once inside, this fades into insignificance as one is enveloped by the hot, steamy atmosphere and the riot of colour and variety. Here, it seems, is every type of exotic plant imaginable, from orchids to palm trees. The man largely responsible for this fine collection was George Forrest, an avid traveller, who brought back hundreds of different plant types from his frequent trips abroad, especially to south-west China. The Glasshouse Experience is one not to be missed – it is a journey to foreign lands, in a world of its own.

Duddingston Loch
HOLYROOD PARK

The village of Duddingston is a curiosity. Although officially a suburb of Edinburgh, it is an independent place that has grown up through the centuries into a quaint and individual collection of buildings, all alive with history. They include the Sheeps Heid, reputedly once frequented by James VI; the twelfth-century church, set on a rocky outcrop above the loch, and the house where Bonnie Prince Charlie held a council of war before the Battle of Prestonpans.

The loch, one of three in Holyrood Park, is now a designated bird sanctuary, and flocks of geese, ducks and coots, among other varieties, have made their homes here. There used to be otters here too, gliding amongst the reeds, but these have now gone, making way for the increasing numbers of birds and other wildlife. In Victorian times, the loch was larger than it is now and was the focal point of the village, attracting people from the surrounding area to admire its tranquillity in the summer months, and to host ice-skating parties during winter.

View of Edinburgh
HOLYROOD PARK

Within the dramatic spread of Holyrood Park is contained a marvellous mixture of landscapes: large areas of wide open space are countered by small glens and woodlands; the harsh outcrops of the Salisbury Crags are scattered with marshlands and lochs. It is a microcosm of the Scottish landscape, represented in an area measuring only 6.4 km (4 miles), and startlingly close to Edinburgh's busy centre.

The whole area was once a great hunting lodge, and it was here that David I was miraculously saved from a charging stag, causing him to found Holyrood Abbey. Although much of it has now been landscaped, the park somehow maintains a wild and romantic air. In 1745, Prince Charles' entire army camped here before setting off on their fatal journey to London. Here too, many of Scotland's monarchs have walked, from the earliest leaders to the more recent royals, in particular Prince Albert, who instigated the creation of St Margaret's Loch, and George VI, who is reputed to have had a special fondness for the place, admiring the beauty of the park and the dramatic nature of the views that enclose it.

St Bernard's Well
DEAN VILLAGE

It is often said that Edinburgh lacks the one element all major cities should have – a river. Although the city and its environs are blessed with an abundance of water in the form of lochs, harbours and the ever-present Firth of Forth, the Water of Leith is its only true claim to a river. The Water, sourced in the Pentland Hills, is hardly a raging torrent – in certain places it is no more than a stream, hardly noticeable amongst the valleys and gorges.

In Dean Village, the old miller's community by the Water of Leith, stands St Bernard's Well. Local legend states that in the twelfth century, during a visit to Scotland, St Bernard of Clairvaux was led by birds to the healing waters of a spring on this spot. In reality, the well was discovered by three boys while fishing in the Water in 1760. The well-water was found to contain minerals and a pump room was soon constructed, with this small Doric temple over it. The statue in the middle portrays Hygieia, the Goddess of Health, and throughout the eighteenth and nineteenth centuries this spot became a popular attraction, not only because of the natural waters, but also because of its beautiful, secluded situation by the calm river waters.

The Meadows
SOUTH EDINBURGH

Hidden behind the University lies another of Edinburgh's many pleasant parks – the Meadows. Like Princes Street Gardens, the area over which the Meadows now stretches was once entirely under water. Known as the South Loch, it used to be the city's main source of water.

By the early eighteenth century, Edinburgh's water was supplied from elsewhere, and plans for a park in this part of town evolved. The loch was drained in 1740, trees were planted and stretches of open grass and woodland sprang up. Paths crossed through the Meadows, and by the late eighteenth century the area had become a fashionable promenade for Edinburgh citizens.

Today, the Meadows are pretty much as they were then, still popular with those seeking the pleasure of open space in the heart of a city. The greens have become common ground for friendly games of cricket and football; the woodland paths and avenues favourites with joggers or those just taking a stroll.

Smug Anchorage
CRAMOND

Cramond is situated at the mouth of the River Almond where it meets the Forth Estuary, and once this was a thriving iron-producing area and milling community, plying its trade via the harbour at the river mouth. At low tide, the whole area is a low, sandy bed and it is possible to walk to the island that lies in the middle, inhabited now only by seabirds. From here, the views across to Fife are spellbinding.

The harbour was also once used as a fishing port, and in its heyday during the eighteenth and nineteenth centuries the village, indeed the whole area, was extremely prosperous. Progress took its toll though, and after the harbour silted up, trading ceased. Now, like Newhaven and Leith, few vessels except pleasure boats anchor here. It remains a charming and historic place. Walks along the banks of the Almond provide the odd reminder of the old trades: remnants of the quarry wharves, relics of the old weirs, mills and cottages.

St Margaret's Loch
HOLYROOD PARK

St Margaret was the grand-niece of Edward the Confessor, but was born exiled in Hungary. In 1054, the Saxon monarchy was re-established and Margaret went to England with her father, to live at Edward's court. After her father died, Margaret's upbringing was left to the austere guidance of Edward, and she did not have a happy youth. With the ascension of King Harold, Margaret decided to return to Hungary, but she got no further than the Firth of Forth, where her ship was wrecked. The English Princess then met the King of Scotland, Malcolm III, whom she married. She died in 1093, three days after hearing of the deaths of her husband and eldest son in battle. The throne passed to her youngest son David I, who was responsible for founding the Abbey at Holyrood. She was canonised in 1249.

It is appropriate then, that this loch situated in Holyrood Park at the foot of Arthur's Seat should be named after her, and that it has royal origins: Prince Albert ordered the loch to be created in an attempt to enhance the beauty of the park. It is a lovely spot, overlooked by the romantic ruins of St Anthony's Chapel, and home to ducks, swans and the famous greylag geese.

Musselburgh Harbour
MUSSELBURGH

The town of Musselburgh takes its name from the many mussel beds that were once found in the River Esk, upon which the town is situated. This was its main source of income for centuries and proved extremely lucrative, causing the harbour to become one of the main fishing and trading ports in the Edinburgh area. It was only in the nineteenth century, when the harbour silted up, that trading diminished.

It is an ancient settlement, dating from Roman times, when a fort was established here to support their camp at Inveresk. The town has seen a victorious Cromwellian army, fresh from the Battle of Dunbar, settle here for a short time, and over the centuries has endured sacking and pillaging by English armies on the march to and from Edinburgh.

Its nickname, the 'Honest Toun', dates from 1332 when Thomas Randolph, Earl of Moray and nephew of Robert the Bruce, was taken ill nearby and was sheltered by the citizens of Musselburgh, away from the invading English, until his death. 'Honest Toun' pageants are still held here annually. Other attractions in Musselburgh include its ancient golf links and racecourse and Pinkie House, the earliest parts of which date from the fourteenth century.

The Port of Leith
LEITH

For many centuries, Leith was separate from Edinburgh, although it was not until 1833 that it became a royal burgh in its own right. The role it has played in Scottish history should not be undervalued, for it was once Scotland's major east coast port.

It was at Leith that Mary, Queen of Scots landed on her joyful return from France to take up her place as monarch of Scotland in 1561. By this time, the port had already suffered much at the hands of the English, having been burned twice in the preceding two decades. It was here also that Cromwell settled his armies for a time during the mid-seventeenth century.

The shipbuilding trade was one of Leith's major industries up until the 1980s, and the remains of this once-thriving port are still in evidence, albeit now in modern terms: the disused warehouses and offices have been turned into exclusive flats, and pubs and bars created from the old buildings abound on the dockside. From here, the ships that sail on a daily basis from the large harbour can be seen embarking on voyages to English and Scandinavian ports, just as they have done for centuries.

Union Canal
EDINBURGH ENVIRONS

In the late eighteenth century, canal-fever swept through Britain. Canals were the ideal method of transporting goods to and from all the major cities, increasing trading potential. In England, these man-made waterways sprung up throughout the country, but in Scotland they were faced with problems: topographically, the country did not invite direct routes and very few of the major cities were far enough away from the coast to warrant canal building.

However, after the construction of the Forth and Clyde Canal, it was decided an extension was needed to enable Lanarkshire coal to reach Scotland's capital and also to transport grain from Edinburgh's milling communities out to Glasgow and the surrounding area. Thus, the Union Canal was born. Stretching 50 km (31 miles) from the Forth and Clyde at Falkirk to a basin ½ mile west of Edinburgh, the Union Canal did not require the construction of any locks, although the valleyed regions needed several aqueducts, some of which survive today.

The Forth and Clyde and the Union Canals were rendered obsolete – like most others in Britain – with the advent of the railways. Today, pleasure cruises along its picturesque stretch are enjoyed, and anglers make the most of the solitude, all a far cry from the trading traffic that once filled the canal.

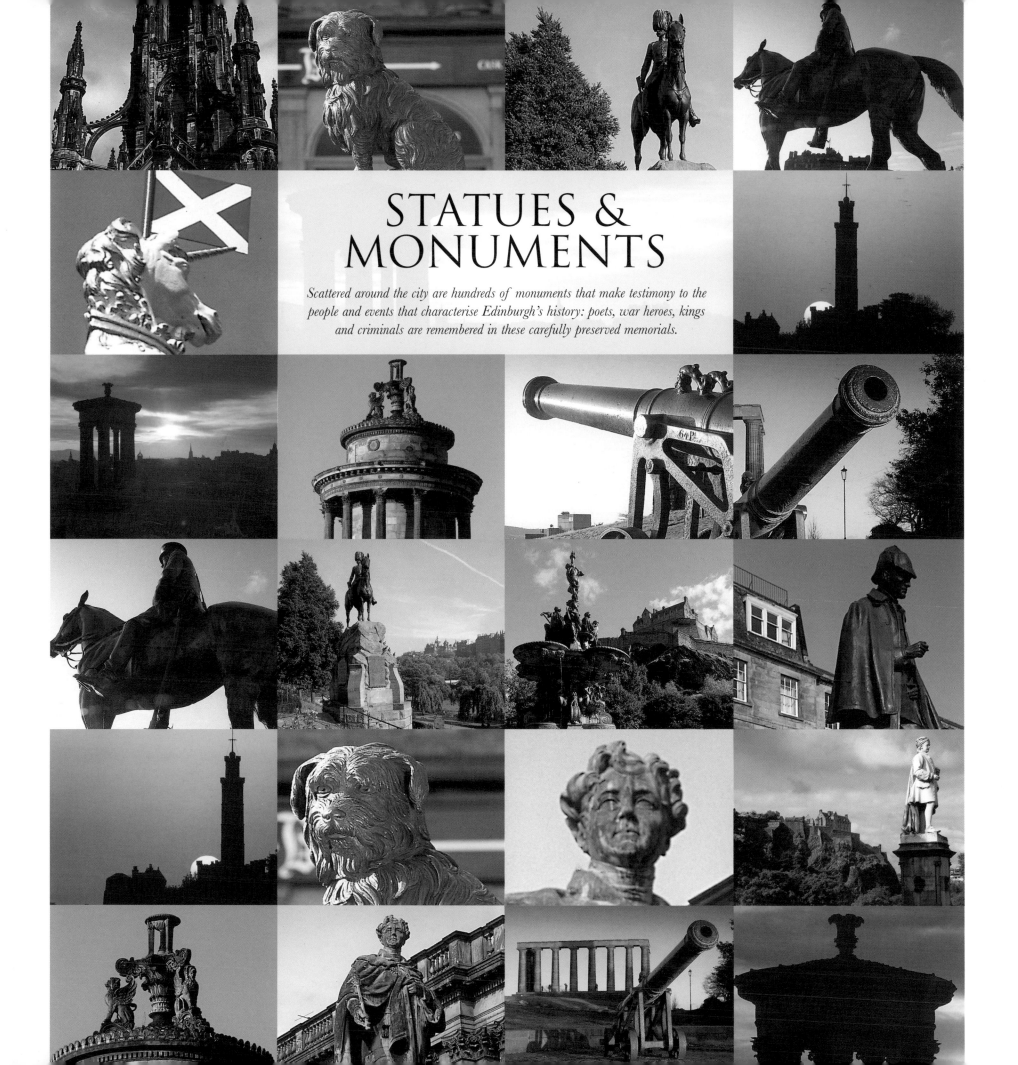

STATUES & MONUMENTS

Scattered around the city are hundreds of monuments that make testimony to the people and events that characterise Edinburgh's history: poets, war heroes, kings and criminals are remembered in these carefully preserved memorials.

National Monument
CALTON HILL

The greatest and strangest of all the monuments scattered across Calton Hill is the National Monument; a half-built Greek temple that gives no indication of its meaning or symbolism. This grand and ambiguous structure was designed by William Playfair in 1822. Intended as a commemoration of the recently ended Napoleonic Wars, Playfair turned to the Scottish love of classical architecture for inspiration for his design, reproducing the Parthenon to Athena, Goddess of War.

Despite lacking sufficient funds to build the monument, work began. It was, needless to say, a difficult task – the huge blocks of stone had to be transported from the quarry outside the city all the way up Calton Hill. By 1829, the money ran out and building stopped. Over the next few years, many suggestions were made as to the uses to which the building could be put, including an art gallery and even the new home for Scottish Parliament. In the event, nothing was decided upon and the monument was left, a massive, half-finished and mysterious object, the purpose of which there appears to be no rhyme or reason.

Memorial to the Royal Scots Greys
PRINCES STREET GARDENS

Set on roughly hewn blocks of sandstone, this bronze equestrian statue is a memorial to the Royal Scots Greys, the oldest regiment in the British Army; one with a reputation for great courage in the face of adversity: the roll of honours listed here bears testimony to this. The statue was erected in 1906 and is the work of Birnie Rhind.

Situated at the east end of Princes Street Gardens, this is one of many monuments that can be found in the Gardens. Many statues line the north side of the boundaries, along the busy line of Princes Street, and scattered around the Gardens are numerous and varied testimonials to a diverse range of people. These include Allan Ramsay, the poet, and Dr James Simpson, the first person to use chloroform as an anaesthetic. Small and discreet, or large and flamboyant, the statues in the Gardens encapsulate the many facets of Edinburgh's intellectual and social history.

Nelson Monument
CALTON HILL

The Scottish have a talent for designing and building imaginative memorials. On Calton Hill alone there is a collection of monuments that seems to defy logic or explanation, and the five-storeyed circular tower that is the Nelson Monument is one of the most peculiar. Built in 1807 shortly after Nelson's death at the Battle of Trafalgar, this is one of the earlier of the hill's buildings and is a curious commemoration of the great naval hero.

The tower stretches over 30 metres (100 ft) high, and its most fascinating feature is the time ball at the top. Every day at one o'clock, this time ball drops in exact synchronisation with the one o'clock gun that is set off across the city at the castle battery. This was once used as a visual time signal to ships in the Firth of Forth, but is now a major tourist attraction. It is certainly worth the climb to the top of the monument, because from here the views over the Forth, the city and out to the horizon, enveloping the dramatic Salisbury Crags, are spectacular.

The Mercat Cross
HIGH STREET

The Mercat Cross on the Royal Mile marks the centre of Old Edinburgh, and has played a vital role in the city's official life. The old high Cross stood in the middle of the High Street in medieval times, and was rebuilt twice before being moved to its present position outside the west door of the High Kirk of St Giles in 1885. The most important ceremony carried out here is the Royal Proclamation: for centuries, royal announcements have been made from here and still are today, accompanied by a fanfare from the Lord Lyon King of Arms. Legend has it that the Cross flowed with wine when the return of Mary, Queen of Scots was declared. Civic proclamations are also made here, most recently the announcement of devolution.

The Cross has a darker history, too. For hundreds of years, executions took place nearby, including that of the great military hero the Marquis of Montrose. Just prior to the infamous Battle of Flodden in 1513, a ghost is said to have stood at the Cross and announced the names of those who would meet their doom in the ensuing fight.

Dugald Stewart Monument
CALTON HILL

The first of the many and varied monuments reached after ascending Calton Hill, this is a memorial to Dugald Stewart (1753 –1828). Like many of Edinburgh's other buildings and monuments, including the Burns Monument (see page 136) and the National Monument (see page 130), this has Grecian echoes, modelled on the Choragic Monument of Lysicrates in Athens.

But who was Dugald Stewart? All over Edinburgh, well-known historical figures – political, literary and royal – are paid tribute to in a marvellous assortment of statues and monuments, but this stately construction – by William Playfair – is something of a curiosity. A Professor of Philosophy at Edinburgh University, Dugald Stewart was a pioneer in his field and had a widespread reputation in his time, his lectures drawing crowds of students eager to hear him expound his latest theories. Unfortunately, time and the ever-changing trends in modern thought and philosophy have rendered his work and reputation obsolete, and he is now a little-known figure outside academic circles. Perhaps though, this attractive memorial will ensure that the he is never entirely forgotten and may one day revive the interest and appreciation of one of the pioneers of modern thought.

Greyfriars Bobby
GREYFRIARS

Amongst the most famous of Edinburgh's citizens is the small Skye terrier known as Greyfriars Bobby, whose life-size statue stands outside Greyfriars Kirkyard on the south side of the Royal Mile.

When his master, John Gray, died in 1858 Bobby followed the procession to the interment in Greyfriars and then refused to leave. At first he was fed by scraps from local kitchens, but soon his fame spread and people would travel to the kirkyard just to see the loyal little dog, ever vigilant at his master's grave. The local people even put up a special shelter for him. He won the hearts not only of the people of Edinburgh, but also the hearts of people the world over as his story spread. Even the Lord Provost of the city at the time paid Bobby's license fee, so that he would not be taken away as a stray.

For 14 years Greyfriars Bobby was never far from John Gray's grave, and when the terrier himself died in 1872, he was laid to rest within the kirkyard near the master he loved so dearly. A year later, this bronze effigy of Bobby was unveiled in testimony to his loyalty and to the sentimental hold his story had – and still has – on visitors and locals.

Ross Fountain

PRINCES STREET GARDENS

The Ross Fountain is one of Princes Street Gardens' more controversial pieces of ornamentation. It is a glorious gilded and impressively large creation that stands in the middle of the park, somewhat out of place amidst the stately landscaped lawns and neat flower beds.

It was created for the 1862 Paris Exhibition and once the Exhibition was finished, the piece was bought by one Daniel Ross, an Edinburgh native, who presented it to the city. It was a noble gesture, but unfortunately not universally pleasing, and the fountain was placed in the Gardens, as hidden away as possible. Perhaps the extravagantly carved, voluptuous figures were rather too much for Victorian sensibilities; they certainly shocked some of the locals, causing the minister at nearby St John's Church to expound that the fountain was 'grossly indecent and disgusting'.

A century later it can be appreciated for what it is – a fine piece of flamboyant experimentation – and the talking point of the Princes Street Gardens!

Sherlock Holmes Statue
PICARDY PLACE

This fine statue of the fictional detective Sherlock Holmes may seem more at home in London's Baker Street than in an unassuming corner of Edinburgh, but its presence here is not altogether unwarranted. Holmes' creator Sir Arthur Conan Doyle was born here at number 11 Picardy Place, and studied medicine at the University of Edinburgh.

The statue was erected in 1991 and was commissioned by the Federation of Master Builders in Edinburgh as a celebration of their fiftieth anniversary. The man responsible for its creation was Gerald Ogilvie Laing, and surprisingly is the only statue of Sherlock Holmes to be found in Britain. Sadly, Conan Doyle's birthplace no longer exists, so it is especially appropriate that he is commemorated here in some way.

The statue is not the only sculpture in this part of the city. A short walk away are some less classical pieces sculpted by Sir Edouardo Paolozzi, Her Majesty's Sculptor-in-Ordinary in Scotland. These bronze pieces include a huge hand and foot, and it is worth a trip to cast a wondering eye over them.

The Scott Monument
PRINCES STREET

The Scott Monument is Edinburgh's most famous memorial, and it is dedicated to its most famous literary son – Sir Walter Scott.

Towering at the east end of Princes Street Gardens, the magnificent Gothic spire of the Scott Monument dominates the vista in this part of the city. Built in 1840 with funds drawn from public subscription, the 67 metre (220 ft) monument was the design of George Meikle Kemp, who sadly did not live to see his masterpiece – and only architectural work – completed. Much thought went into the design, however, and it is a fitting testimony. At every level of the age-blackened spire representations of Scottish writers and characters from Scott's novels are intricately carved. It is a complete three-dimensional résumé of the works of Scotland's best-loved writer.

At the base of the monument sits a Carrara marble statue of Scott himself, with his dog Maida. This is the inspiration of Sir John Steell, a perfect complement to the lofty spire. The Scott Monument, the largest and most ambitious memorial to a writer ever constructed, is the focus of the New Town and Edinburgh's pride in it echoes the nation's pride in the man to whom it is dedicated.

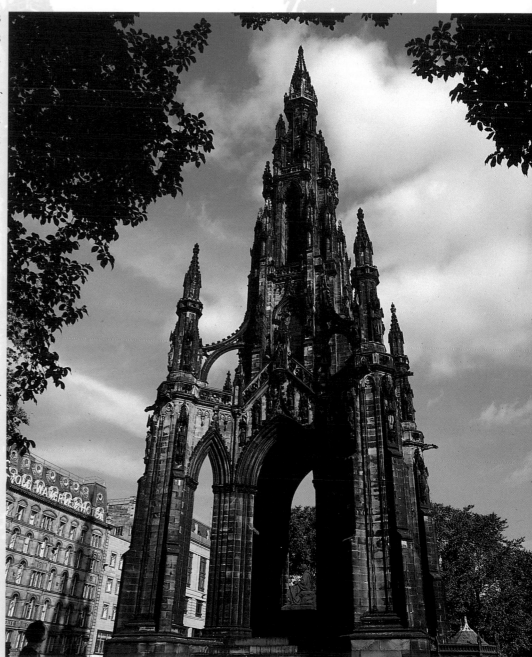

Burns Monument
REGENT ROAD

Is there a Bard of rustic song,
Who, noteless, steals the crouds among,
That weekly this area throng,
O, pass not by!
But with a frater-feeling strong,
Here, heave a sigh.

Although Robert Burns was not an Edinburgher by birth, his status as national bard undoubtedly earns him a memorial in his country's capital. Like the monument to Dugald Stewart on the nearby Calton Hill, the Burns Monument is a simplified replica of the Monument to Lysicrates in Athens, reflecting the Scots love of classical Greek architecture. A two-staged, cylindrical-columned structure, it was erected in 1830 at the foot of the Royal Mile in Regent Road.

The Burns Monument was once enhanced by a statue of the poet at its base. Sadly, this has been taken away, and although it can still be admired in the National Portrait Gallery, its loss somehow detracts from the significance of the small Corinthian temple erected in Burn's honour.

Statue of George IV
GEORGE STREET

George Street was intended to be one of the main thoroughfares in the New Town, running from St Andrew's Square and Charlotte Square, parallel to Princes Street. Craig, the chief designer and architect of the New Town, planned this stately avenue to be the city's residential heart. Today, there are no private residences along this stretch, the fine houses have all been turned into offices and the street is now the financial centre of Edinburgh, the equivalent of the City of London. The buildings, however, stand as a reminder of the way Edinburgh's wealthier residents once lived.

Standing tall on a granite pedestal, the regal statue of George IV, designed by Chantrey, was unveiled in 1831 – a year after the King's death – and stands at the crossing of Hanover Street. Here, the monarch surveys the architectural triumph of the Royal Scottish Academy and the picturesque rise of The Mound, looking south towards the Old Town. George IV paid a visit to Edinburgh in 1822, and certainly made an impression on the Scottish people by parading around the Palace of Holyroodhouse in his tartan kilt.

Memorial Cannon
CALTON HILL

The cannon on Calton Hill is one of the most photographed monuments in Edinburgh, yet it is also one of the most obscure and little of its history is readily accessible.

It is believed to have been built sometime before 1624, the date inscribed on the barrel, and is almost certainly Portuguese. It came to Edinburgh via Burma, where it must have seen some action – a Burmese inscription on the cannon reinforces this. It was captured by the British during the Conquest of Burma in 1886, and taken as a memento of the Mandalay Campaign. After being transported to Britain it was presented as a gift to the City of Edinburgh, and put on show at the Meadows International Exhibition in the same year. It then joined the collection of monuments that grace the summit of Calton Hill.

During the Second World War, many of Edinburgh's metal memorials were taken away to be melted down into ammunition, and for a while this hard-won monument was in danger of playing a less dramatic role in another campaign. However, due to its long history and a local public outcry, it was left in state on the hill, an unusual and ambiguous piece of British history.

Statue of Allan Ramsay
PRINCES STREET GARDENS

It has been suggested that it is degrading for one of Edinburgh's most eminent citizens to be immortalised in a statue wearing his nightcap, but in Allan Ramsay's time (1686–1758), such items were considered fashionable, and it seems unlikely that the poet would have minded – he was renowned for his good humour.

It is, perhaps, an appropriate reminder of his origins as a wig maker, a profession he abandoned to become a bookseller in 1718. From this grew his passion and talent for literature, in particular poetry. He began to publish collections of poetry, including the *Tea Table Miscellany* which brought together many Scottish songs and ballads, and later was an inspiration for Robert Burns, amongst others.

Ramsay's own works began to appear sporadically around 1721, but it was not until 1725's *The Gentle Shepherd* that he began to receive real critical acclaim. This pastoral work became one of the most popular Scots works of its time. Shortly afterwards, Ramsay established the first library in Britain.

This statue, carved from Carrara marble by Sir John Steell, was erected in 1865. It stands in a prime position at the crossroads of Princes Street and The Mound, reflecting Ramsay's contribution to the Scots' literary world.

Statue of Field Marshal Haig
CASTLE ESPLANADE, CASTLEHILL

There are a number of objects of interest that stand on the Castle Esplanade, a curious collection of reminders of Edinburgh's past. The most fascinating, and macabre, is the drinking fountain in the north-east corner. Art nouveau in style, this is made up of images of witches and serpents and marks the place where local women accused of witchcraft, met a horrific end. Hundreds of women were burned at the stake here throughout the fifteenth, sixteenth and seventeenth centuries.

Not far away from here stands this beautifully cast, bronze equestrian statue of Field Marshal Haig. Haig, an Edinburgher by birth, was commander of the British troops during the First World War. When this statue was unveiled in 1923 in the aftermath of the allied victory, Haig was something of a national hero. His radical front-line strategies, however, have since been looked at with hindsight, and controversy still surrounds his methods of fighting.

The Palace of Holyroodhouse
CANONGATE

The processional stretch of the Royal Mile leads eventually to the gates of the magnificent Palace of Holyroodhouse, home of kings past and present, and alive with the ghosts of Edinburgh's history.

The massive wrought-iron gates open on to a suitably regal forecourt from which rises the impressive stone palace. It was built under the orders of James IV in 1498, although little of the original building is left today. Fifty years after its construction, the palace suffered serious damage by the Earl of Hertford's troops and a century later Cromwell's army left their own mark on it. By the time the monarchy was restored, there was little left of the grand palace that Holyrood had once been.

In the 1670s, Charles II ordered the palace to be restored, and Sir William Bruce redesigned and reconstructed large parts of the building. In the event, Charles II never even visited Holyrood to appreciate the marvellous craftsmanship, but we have him to thank for the continued existence of this royal home.

Carving
PALACE OF HOLYROODHOUSE, CANONGATE

This carved relief of the royal arms is found above the main entrance to Holyrood. A visit to the palace is like taking a journey through the capital's turbulent history. The rich surroundings enhance the atmosphere of ancient and dramatic events, where Scotland's kings and queens have lived and died.

James V's tower is the oldest surviving part of the palace and Mary, Queen of Scots' own apartments were on the second floor. Here she held court with some of Edinburgh's most distinguished figures, including John Knox (whom she later accused of treason). Here also, the queen undertook her unwise union with Bothwell after the murder of her husband Lord Darnley. The queen's secretary Rizzio was murdered in the palace in one of the most infamous incidents in Scottish royal history, and a plaque marks the exact spot where this took place. On a lighter note, in another part of the palace is the long Picture Gallery, which contains no less than 111 portraits of Scottish kings and queens by the Dutch painter Jacob de Wit, most of which, however, are based more on legend than fact.

Tantallon Castle
NEAR DIRLETON

Surrounded on three sides by the sea crashing on the rocks below, and on the fourth by a moat, it is not difficult to gauge Tantallon's strategic importance in medieval times. The Castle has seen more military action than any other fortification around Edinburgh, except perhaps Edinburgh Castle.

Built at the end of the fourteenth century, it was the home of one of Scotland's most notorious clans – the Douglas family, the Earls of Angus – for many years. One of the greatest sieges laid on Tantallon Castle was led by the young James V. The Sixth Earl of Angus held a great deal of power and sway in the early 1500s and while the king was in his minority, the earl used his influence to keep him a virtual prisoner in the city. On achieving his majority James V charged Angus with treason and launched an assault on the Douglas family stronghold. It is a testimony to the strength of Tantallon's construction that, although James was the ultimate victor in the battle, it was as a result of lengthy negotiation rather than the strength of his attack. Douglas escaped abroad, and James V took ownership of the castle.

This magnificent fortification was eventually destroyed by Cromwell in 1651 after a 12-day siege and was never repaired, its remnants now standing as an eerie reminder of Scotland's violent history.

Dirleton Castle
DIRLETON

The extensive ruins of the Castle are the dominant feature of the village of Dirleton. The original castle was built in the thirteenth century by the de Vaux family and parts of this still remain, most notably the Lord's Hall, a room that despite its decayed state, still reflects some of its former majesty. The Castle was later extended and modified by the Halyburton family, who added the Great Hall. Later owners also included the infamous Ruthven family, members of which were involved in the murder of Mary, Queen of Scots' favourite Rizzio.

Dirleton Castle's best-known resident was the tragic Dorothea, wife of the Earl of Gowrie. Gowrie was a rebellious man, and after his part in a conspiracy to attack Stirling Castle was discovered, James VI confiscated all his family lands and possessions, including the Castle, had the unfortunate earl executed and left his even more unfortunate widow and 15 children destitute. Dorothea survived until the castle and lands were restored to her a few years later, but the story does not have a happy ending. It seems her sons had inherited their father's rebellious nature and after the involvement of two of them in the 'Gowrie Conspiracy' – a mysterious affair whose aim seemed to be the king's assassination – Dorothea was once again left destitute.

Blackness Castle
NEAR SOUTH QUEENSFERRY

When the Act of Union was passed in 1707, Blackness Castle was one of only four castles in Scotland permitted to maintain their fortifications – an indication of its strategic and historical importance.

Surrounded on three sides by the Forth, and jutting out on a rocky promontory, Blackness is one of the most dramatic and mysterious sights around Edinburgh. The castle's original date is unknown, and the tower that remains today almost certainly dates from the fifteenth century, but the rest of the castle may be even earlier. The tower is likely to have been an additional fortification built when the castle was a major fortress. It has witnessed some great events, including a siege by Cromwell, but by the seventeenth century was being used as a state prison, and its fortunes declined from this time until in the nineteenth century, it eventually became no more than a storage for gunpowder. Today it is a relic, but one of the darkest and most dramatic relics Edinburgh has to offer.

Craigmillar Castle
NEAR DUDDINGSTON

In the sixteenth century Craigmillar Castle was situated beyond the boundaries of Edinburgh, although today its site just south-east of Duddingston village makes it very much a part of the city. It became a favourite spot for Mary, Queen of Scots during her reign, and many tales associated with the castle are related to the unfortunate queen. Mary's father, James V, made this his home for a short while in 1517, and after large-scale damage was inflicted by the English Earl of Hertford, the castle was rebuilt to provide Mary with a place of refuge. She fled here after the brutal murder of her secretary Rizzio in 1566, and local legend states that it was here at Craigmillar that the plot to murder Lord Darnley was hatched the following year.

Although its fame dates back to the sixteenth century Craigmillar is much older than this. Some of its surviving parts were constructed during the fourteenth century, including the tower house. By the middle of the seventeenth century, the whole west wing had been renovated and turned into an unusual stately home, but a hundred years on, the place was evacuated and has been uninhabited ever since. The sprawling ruins are some of the most fantastic in Edinburgh.

Dalmeny House
NEAR SOUTH QUEENSFERRY

The site of Dalmeny House has been the seat of the Earls of Roseberry for three centuries. The current house dates from 1815, and is the handiwork of William Wilkins – a magnificent example of neo-Gothic architecture, absorbed into an impressive, but imposing, pile – around which stretch landscaped gardens and parkland.

The interior of Dalmeny House is in keeping with its style: from the fine hammerbeam hall to the furniture and furnishing, everything complements everything else in a Gothic feast in the Scottish style. Dalmeny's biggest attraction is its fine collection of paintings, and the portraits include works by Reynolds, Gainsborough and Edinburgh's own Raeburn. The most unusual feature is the Napoleon Room, an exhibition given over to items and pieces of memorabilia that once belonged to the great French General. These were collected by the fifth Earl of Roseberry, who extravagantly indulged his fascination of the nineteenth-century hero.

Edinburgh Castle
CASTLEHILL

Edinburgh Castle has been destroyed and rebuilt a number of times since its construction as a hunting lodge by Malcolm III in the eleventh century. Little now remains from this period, the oldest surviving part of the castle being St Margaret's Chapel, dating from the twelfth century.

The first major structural changes to the castle were made in 1313, when the Scots finally recaptured the castle from the English. In order to prevent their old enemy from ever being able to use it as a defence, the king ordered that it be dismantled. It was rebuilt half a century later under the orders of David II. From this time it developed into the city's major asset, playing the role of royal palace as well as central focus of military defence. It saw its last true military action during Bonnie Prince Charlie's brief residence in 1745. After this, its role as a fortification declined.

Penicuik House
PENICUIK

The town of Penicuik, situated at the foot of the rolling Pentland Hills, is just within the southern limit of Edinburgh's boundaries, and the ruins of Penicuik House are the main feature of the town.

The house was built to designs by Sir James Clerk in 1778, whose father had played a large part in the creation of the grounds – the House's most splendid feature. These are liberally scattered with thousands of trees and a plethora of buildings such as pavilions, bridges and watchtowers, an eighteenth-century trait. When Sir John died in 1755, his son continued his work, completing the collection of monuments with a Chinese gate and an obelisk. These creations make for a fascinating journey through the grounds, providing an insight into contemporary architectural trends.

The house itself is typical Scots Palladian, and the grandeur of its style can still be appreciated, despite the fact it was all but destroyed by a fire at the turn of the nineteenth century. The House was never properly rebuilt, and the nearby stables were converted into the family home – an unusual and picturesque residence adjacent to the ruins.

Hopetoun House
NEAR SOUTH QUEENSFERRY

Two architects were mainly responsible for the magnificence of Hopetoun House: Sir William Bruce and William Adam. Bruce designed the earlier part of the house at the turn of the eighteenth century, and the excellent interior carvings and ceiling paintings are all part of his complete vision. In 1721, Adam extended Hopetoun, enhancing its grandeur with the addition of a palatial façade and the rooms now known as the State Apartments. Another significant feature of the house is the unusual rooftop platform, from which the views of the Firth and the surrounding countryside are unsurpassed. The works of each of these architects complement each other in a harmonious, perfectly unified whole and together they have created arguably the most impressive stately home on the shores of the Firth.

Since it was built, Hopetoun has been the seat of the Earls of Hopetoun, and part of the house is still occupied by them. Fortunately, the public have a free rein around the rest of the house, and can wander amongst the exquisite interiors – mainly attributable to Adam – which are a suitable reflection of eighteenth-century high society.

Linlithgow Palace
LINLITHGOW

On the edge of the beautiful Linlithgow Loch lie the evocative ruins of Linlithgow Palace, where history echoes through the cavernous rooms and around the ancient walls. A long line of Scottish monarchs has an association with Linlithgow: David I first built a manor house here in the twelfth century, although the present palace dates from the time of James I. One of the most tragic tales associated with the palace tells how Queen Margaret stood at the top of the north-west tower watching for her husband James IV to return from the Battle of Flodden in 1513. The legend also tells how James was told his fate by a ghostly apparition in the nearby St Michael's Church. Margaret, of course, waited in vain.

James V and Mary, Queen of Scots were both born at Linlithgow; Charles I stayed here in 1633 and Bonnie Prince Charlie passed through a century later, shortly followed by the Duke of Cumberland and his troops who, in their eager pursuit of the Jacobite rebels, left the fires burning, reducing the palace to the massive, awe-inspiring ruins it is today.

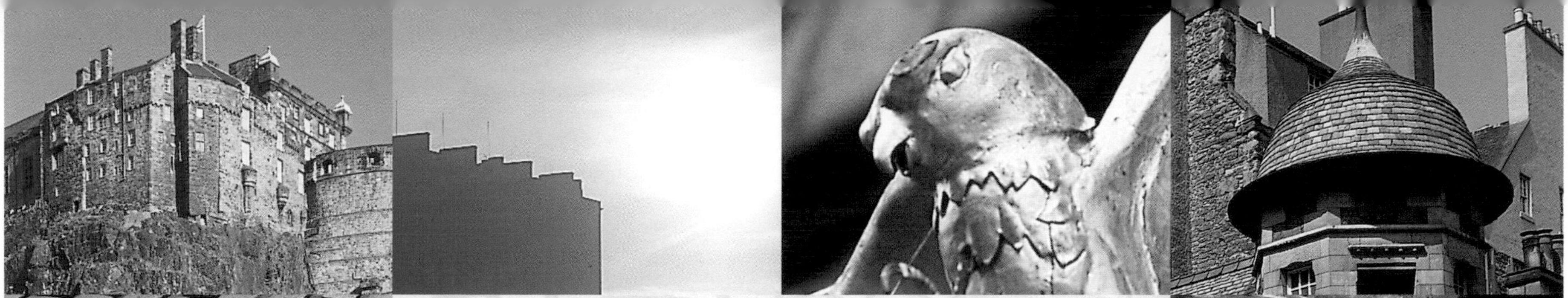

HISTORIC EDINBURGH

Throughout the city and its suburbs lie numerous museums and other buildings that tell the tale of Edinburgh's rich history. All serve as a reminder of some of the city's greatest events and as a testimony to its most colourful characters.

BRODIE'S TAVERN

HUNT

FOR WE ARE VERY LUCKY WITH A LAMP BEFORE THE DOOR,
AND LEERIE STOPS TO LIGHT IT AS HE LIGHTS SO MANY MORE;
AND O! BEFORE YOU HURRY BY WITH LADDER AND WITH LIGHT,
O LEERIE, SEE A LITTLE CHILD AND NOD TO HIM TONIGHT!

THE PEOPLE'S STORY

Gladstone's Land
LAWNMARKET

In 1617, one Thomas Gledstane bought a humble property on the site of the house that now bears his name. As his fortunes grew, this small house was extended and modified until it became a fine example of a seventeenth-century merchant's home. Rising to a height of six storeys, the Gledstane family did not occupy the whole building, confining themselves to the third floor and increasing their wealth by renting out the rest of their home.

All six storeys have now been carefully restored to represent the style of Gledstane's era and the museum gives a good idea of how the prosperous middle classes would once have lived in Edinburgh. Keeping to the theme of the merchant classes, there are a number of exhibits showing the kind of goods that would have been traded in the seventeenth century, including magnificent collections of pottery and porcelain, and the style of the interior is accurate rather than overwhelmingly opulent. Particularly fine are the typical, arcaded ground floor and the hypnotic painted ceilings.

Holyrood Abbey
CANONGATE

Legend tells how King David I was hunting in the woodland that once covered this whole area, when he was attacked by a stag. A silver cloud appeared in the sky, from which descended a holy cross. At the sight of this the stag fled, and in acknowledgement of this miracle, King David founded the Monastery of the Holy Rood. The year was 1128, and it is from this time that Edinburgh's tumultuous religious history grew.

It was not long before the humble monastery had grown into an abbey, and the lives of an illustrious trail of Scottish monarchs became entwined with this place. James II, III and IV were all married in the Abbey; the most famous wedding of all to take place here being that of Mary, Queen of Scots, to the ill-fated Darnley. James V and Charles I were both crowned here, and James III's grave is amongst those numbered here.

The tide of the Reformation was indiscriminate, however, and not even its royal history could save the Abbey from destruction. Subsequent restoration work culminated in the new roof in 1758. Ten years later this gave way, and was never repaired, and eventually the Abbey crumbled into the evocative ruins we see today.

Edinburgh Castle
CASTLEHILL

The first castle was built here by Malcolm III, who intended to use it primarily as a hunting lodge, but there had undoubtedly been some kind of fortification here for centuries. Eventually, Malcolm's lodge grew into the principal home for the Scottish monarchy, and despite regular attacks by the English – sometimes successful, sometimes less so – the Scots managed to win back their greatest asset. The most famous story tells how in 1314, Thomas Randolph, Earl of Moray, scaled the sheer rock face with a group of just 13 men to recapture the castle from the English during the Wars of Independence.

One of the castle's most intriguing unsolved mysteries stems from the discovery in 1830 of a small coffin, containing the remains of a baby wrapped in a silk shroud embroidered with the letter 'J'. This was discovered behind the panelling of the room in which it is known that Mary, Queen of Scots gave birth to James VI. Was this the body of the real heir to the Scottish throne? Like so many other royal mysteries, this will probably never be solved.

The Honours of Scotland
EDINBURGH CASTLE

One of the greatest attractions at the castle is the Crown Room, where Scotland's Crown Jewels are now kept. The crown itself was made for James V, but the gold circlet that has been incorporated into it was actually worn by Robert the Bruce. The oldest piece is the sceptre, adorned with miniature figures of St James and St Andrew, the Virgin Mary and the Christ Child. The third piece, the sword, was created in Italy by Domenico da Sutri and given to James IV by Pope Julius II.

The jewels were first removed from the castle after they had been used in the coronation of Charles II. Enraged by the Restoration, Oliver Cromwell tried to steal them and have them destroyed, but they were smuggled out and hidden just in time. When the danger had passed, they were returned to the castle, where they remained until the Act of Union in 1707, after which they were put away. After a few years, it was generally accepted that Scotland's Crown Jewels were lost forever, but in 1818, following a search instigated by Sir Walter Scott, they were rediscovered, locked in a chest in a small room in the castle. Since then they have been on display for all to admire.

Roman Fort
CRAMOND

Cramond's strategic importance is obvious from its location at the mouth of the River Almond and the Firth of Forth, and the village name means 'fort on the river'. It had been known for many years that Cramond was an ancient site, dating back far beyond its eighteenth-century heyday, and relics from Roman times have been periodically discovered here. It was only in 1954, however, that the foundations of this Roman fort were uncovered.

This area was once the northernmost line of the Roman frontier, and the fort would have been constructed as a protection for the harbour down below, which was vital for survival to the Romans whose supply ships would have docked here. It was built in AD 142 by order of Emperor Antonius Pius, although the evidence suggests that it was abandoned shortly afterwards. Emperor Septimus Severus rebuilt the fort early in the third century as a head-quarters from which he planned his attack on the north-east of Scotland. Low walls now outline the various buildings which include barracks, workshops, the line of the ramparts, the headquarters and the 'via principalis'.

Old Royal High School
REGENT ROAD

O f all the buildings in Edinburgh inspired by classical Greek architecture, the Old Royal High School is indisputably the finest. The brainchild of Thomas Hamilton, its design was based on the Temple of Theseus in Athens, and it is a fantastic, sprawling collection of pavilions and colonnades. Its setting could not be more impressive either, its lofty position commanding views of Arthur's Seat.

The idea for a new school belonged to the City Fathers, who intended it to be the city's finest educational establishment. Work began on the school in 1825 and was finally completed in 1829. In the course of its history it has educated many of Edinburgh's most famous sons, among them Robert Adam and Alexander Graham Bell.

The building ceased being a school in the 1960s and since then has been used for a number of temporary purposes, including the Crown Office Headquarters and the Prosecution service in Scotland.

Gateway
GRASSMARKET

The Grassmarket is, as its name suggests, an ancient market place, where farmers would sell their hay and seeds. But over the centuries, it grew into one of Edinburgh's most notorious areas, and has been the scene of numerous crimes, rebellions and murders.

It was one of the main sites for public executions, and a cross in the market place remembers the many Covenanters who were martyred here. The last recorded public execution took place in the Grassmarket at the end of the eighteenth century, by which time hundreds of unhappy Edinburghers had lost their lives.

The most famous tale associated with the Grassmarket is that of the notorious body snatchers Burke and Hare. This, the seamiest area of Old Edinburgh, was their haunt. This infamous pair would walk the Grassmarket area looking for victims, who they would ply with alcohol and then strangle, selling the bodies for a tidy sum to Robert Knox, a respectable medical professor at the University, who then used the bodies to teach his students the principles of dissection. Whether or not he had his suspicions as to the dubious origins of this steady supply of cadavers is not known. Burke and Hare were finally caught, and Burke was hanged on the evidence of his unscrupulous partner in crime.

Robert Louis Stevenson's House
HERIOT ROW

The Stevenson family lived in Heriot Row in Edinburgh's New Town from 1857, when the young Robert was just seven years old. Stevenson later followed in the family tradition by studying engineering at the University, but felt no calling for this vocation and switched instead to law. At the same time he began to spend more and more time mixing with the 'low life' of the Old Town. It was from this that he gained much inspiration for his later novels. By the time he was called to the Bar in 1875, Stevenson had decided that his future lay in writing.

He left his comfortable middle-class home in Heriot Row in 1879 determined to see the world, and hopefully find a place more suitable for his weak constitution than the damp Scottish climate. He went first to France, where he met his future wife, Fanny Osbourne, and then on to Switzerland. He returned to Scotland – to the Highlands – for a while, but eventually left for good, visiting America and finally making his home in Samoa, where he died in 1894.

Despite his travels, Stevenson never forgot his early influences, and his love for Scotland and the great impression both the country and its people had on him are reflected in his writing.

The Heart of Midlothian
HIGH STREET

Outlined in cobbled stones just outside the High Kirk of St Giles, is the Heart of Midlothian, marking the site where the Old Tolbooth used to stand: the town prison and place of execution. This building was known as the 'Heart of Midlothian', and was a dark and dreary building, as such a place would be. It was here that many a notorious figure took their final bow.

Throughout the centuries, the Old Tolbooth, which was built in 1466 and extended in the next century, has served many civic purposes. Its original use was as a chapter house for St Giles, then in a perhaps more distinguished role, it played host for some years to parliamentary meetings and served as a somewhat lowly law court. It was only later that it adopted its new title as city prison.

The building has long since disappeared, but the heart-shaped memorial in the road serves as a reminder of the different ages in Edinburgh's past, some more illustrious than others. It is a tradition in the city, incidentally, to spit on the Heart of Midlothian, a ritual that is supposed to bring good luck.

Canongate Tolbooth (The People's Story)
CANONGATE

This remarkably well-preserved building dates from the sixteenth century. Its unassuming and orderly aspect, complete with clock and tower, however, reveals little of the building's history. This was once the administrative heart of the Canongate, back in the days when this part of the city was a separate burgh. Here in centuries past, the town council met and made all the decisions most affecting Edinburgh's citizens. Here the law courts held session and here also, in the eighteenth century, those unfortunate enough to be found guilty were imprisoned. Unlike its earlier counterpart further up the Royal Mile, near St Giles, this was one of the better prisons: cleaner, and less dark, dingy and disease-ridden and, it appears, was reserved for a higher order of prisoner. Historian Hugo Arnot wrote in 1777: 'Debtors of a better sort are commonly taken to this prison, which is well aired, has some decent rooms, and is kept tolerably clean.'

Today, this marvellous building houses the 'People's Story', a museum recounting the lives of the ordinary citizens of Edinburgh over the past two centuries.

Inchcolm Abbey
THE FIRTH OF FORTH

The tranquil island of Inchcolm lies about 4.8 km (3 miles) out in the Firth of Forth, and is now uninhabited. It was once the site of a thriving and industrious abbey, however, and its romantic remains are a marvellous spectacle on this otherwise deserted island.

An Augustinian priory was established here by Alexander I in 1123. His ship had been wrecked in the Forth nearby, and the king was helped by the hermit who lived on Inchcolm. Alexander founded the priory in recognition and gratitude for this help. A century later it was elevated to the status of abbey. Even out here, though, the religious settlement could not escape the effects of the Reformation, when it was largely destroyed by the English. It was restored in later times, and some parts of the original building remain. These include a small church and a chapter house. The other site of interest on Inchcolm is a cave in the north of the island, which some claim to have been the hermit's abode, although this is largely speculation.

Lady Stair's House
(The Writer's Museum)
LAWNMARKET

Lady Stair was a great society figure in the eighteenth century, and a great character too, by all accounts. She was married to Viscount Primrose, but she was left a widow while still a young woman, and she embarked upon her second marriage to the Earl of Stair, a colonel of the Royal Scots Greys and a society gentleman overfond of the bottle. Lady Stair was an admirable match for him though, reputedly taking pleasure from shocking people with bad language and a violent temper. The lintel over the door to the house is therefore somewhat ironic in its inscription which preaches 'Fear The Lord & Depart From Evil'.

The house was built in 1622, but little of its original seventeenth-century character remains due to extensive restorations in the late nineteenth century. Today, the building houses the Writer's Museum, a small and intriguing exhibition of the lives and works of Scotland's greatest literary heroes: Robert Burns, Robert Louis Stevenson and Sir Walter Scott.

Deacon Brodie's Tavern
LAWNMARKET

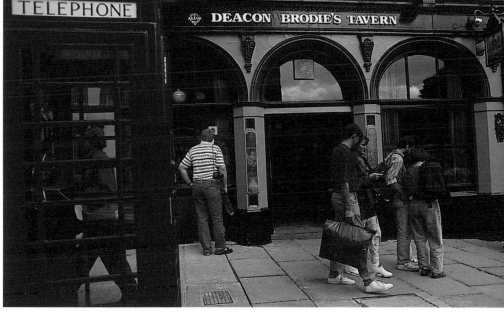

Deacon Brodie's Tavern is just one of the many reminders around the city, particularly the Old Town, of Edinburgh's most notorious villain. It is not uncommon for criminals to become celebrated figures after their lifetimes, and Deacon Brodie's cause was much enhanced by Stevenson's novel *Dr Jekyll and Mr Hyde*, which drew its inspiration from this tale of mystery and intrigue.

William Brodie was, to all appearances, an upstanding member of the community. He held a post as city councillor and was generally highly thought of in respectable circles. Brodie had a darker side, however, and was given to gambling, drinking and womanising. When his trade as a cabinet-

maker began to limit his ability to partake in these activities, Brodie turned to crime. He would make impressions of the house keys of the members of the higher society that he visited in his official capacity, and have replica keys made. In the dead of night, he would then return to the houses and make off with anything of value.

This double life finally caught up with him after a failed robbery at the Excise Office, and he was captured while attempting to flee to America. The final irony of the tale is that when he was hanged in 1788, it was on gallows made by his own company.

Gillespie Plaque
ROYAL MILE

Edinburgh is not only a city of kings and queens, although their stories naturally tend to dominate the city's history. One of the greatest features of Edinburgh is the great diversity of its inhabitants: many noble names are amongst the role of distinguished Edinburghers, but there is also a plethora of lesser known, but none the less interesting, characters whose lives give a broader perspective of Edinburgh's history.

This plaque commemorates James Gillespie of Spylaw, an eighteenth-century merchant native of the city. James and his brother John were both bachelors, and thrifty ones at that. They built themselves an empire in the form of a snuff factory and a retail outlet, which amassed them a modest fortune. When he died, James Gillespie bequeathed this fortune to the city, with instructions that it should be used to build a hospital for old people which, true to his orders, went up in 1802, and a school for poor boys. This, too, was built according to his orders. The old gentleman would probably turn in his grave at the sight of this school today, which is a semi-private establishment.

Huntly House Museum
CANONGATE

There are a number of buildings along the Royal Mile that have been turned into museums of various kinds. Huntly House now houses a collection of exhibits on Edinburgh's local history, which mainly consist of details about local industries, including pottery and clockmaking. The museum's main object of interest, however, is the original National Covenant dating from 1638, which some say was signed in blood, although tests have failed to prove conclusively whether or not this is true.

The building itself has a fascinating history. It is one of the oldest surviving structures along this stretch, dating back to the sixteenth century, when it was a respectable town house. Like so many others, it was virtually destroyed at the hands of the English in 1544, but was carefully restored later in the century. The Incorporation of Hammermen acquired the house in 1647 and turned it into a series of flats, and it remained thus until the nineteenth century when it finally fell into decay. In the early twentieth century the City of Edinburgh took on the job of rebuilding it and in 1927 it opened its doors again, as a museum. It has been carefully maintained since then.

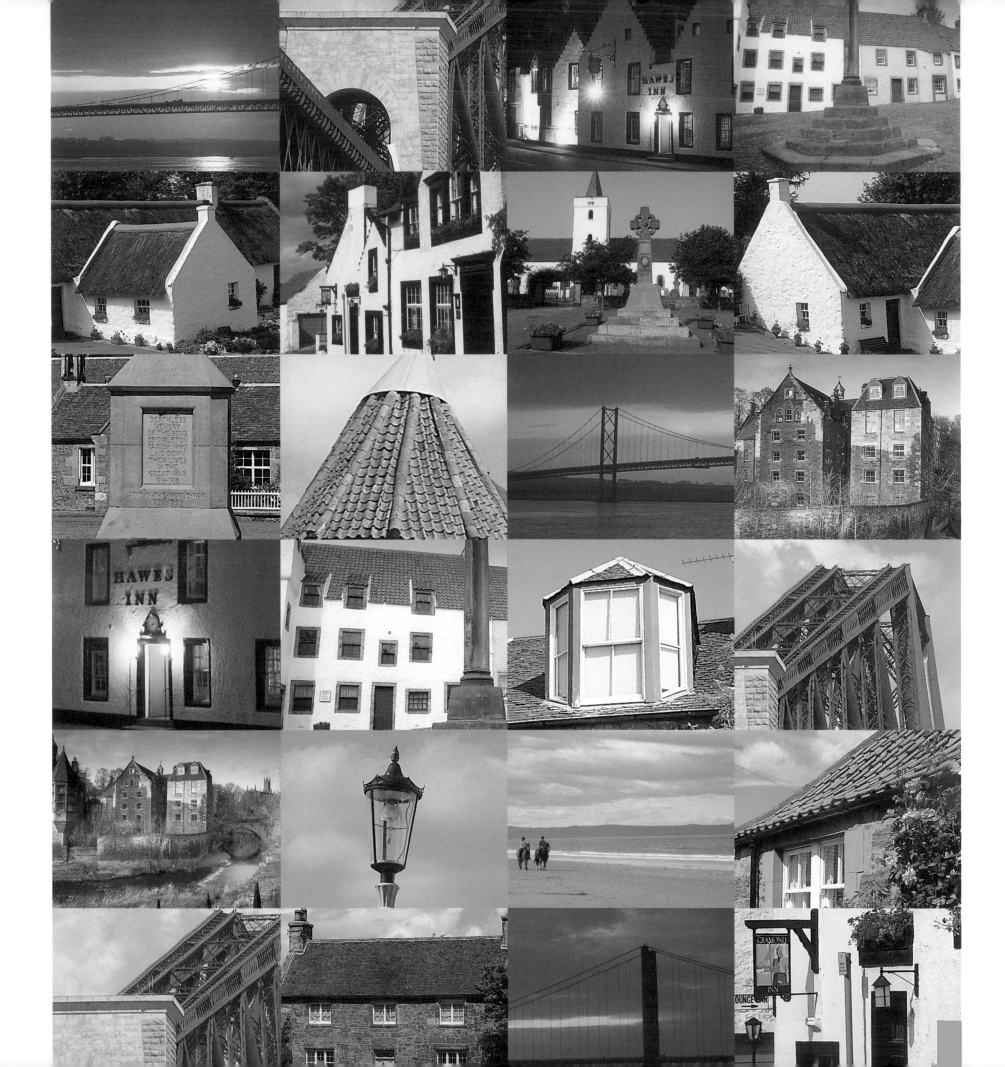

AROUND EDINBURGH

In the countryside that stretches out for miles around Edinburgh lie many picturesque villages and small towns. Each of these places has its own historic tales to tell, of the industry and practices that made up these once-thriving communities.

Cottages
SWANSTON

Nestled at the foot of the Pentland Hills is one of Robert Louis Stevenson's favourite villages – Swanston. The writer spent many summers here at Swanston Cottage, built by his father Thomas, admiring the tranquillity of the village and the views of the nearby city afforded by its situation.

The whitewashed cottages are spread out around the village green, although their thatched roofs are an unusual sight in Scotland. Dating from the seventeenth century, these were once used by the workers of the 'ferm toun', farms that were run by a group of people rather than just one proprietor.

Swanston once had an abundance of clear spring water, and it was from here that, after a lengthy series of legal problems, Edinburgh was finally allowed to supplement its water supply. Although Swanston is lacking in certain amenities – there is neither church nor shop – it retains its traditional charm and beauty.

Main Street
INVERESK

At one time, the parish of Inveresk extended right to the mouth of the River Esk, as the village's name implies. Today, the name applies just to the village itself, but Inveresk is not a place that sprang up around Edinburgh during the seventeenth and eighteenth centuries. It is remarkably ancient, dating back to Roman times, when a fort and settlement grew up in this area, and many relics of these times have been uncovered in and around Inveresk.

Today, however, there is little that associates the village with those far-off, ancient days, for the architecture is undeniably and proudly Georgian in style. Rows of mansion houses rise regally from behind the trees and high walls, dominating the road leading to the manor house. There is little mix here of the larger houses and the typical Scots cottages, for the mansion house owners eventually pushed out the cottagers, and their dwellings ceased to exist. Today, this makes for an unusually rich, luxurious and, dare we say it, upper-class aspect. This culminates in the carefully tended Inveresk Lodge Gardens, set in the grounds of what is now a National Trust House, one of Inveresk's finest features.

The Water of Leith
DEAN VILLAGE

Lying in a valley to the north of Edinburgh's New Town on the banks of the Water of Leith, Dean Village is one of the most attractive spots the area has to offer.

From the twelfth century until late Victorian times, the village was a thriving milling community, with 11 mills powered by the river and two granaries. The Incorporation of Baxters (or bakers) once owned five of the mills here, and their mark – two crossed bakers' shovels carrying loaves – can be seen on some of the houses that still stand by the waters. Sadly, few of the mill buildings still survive, and today the village is a tranquil and undisturbed spot, a far cry from the hub of industry it was for over 700 years.

It is, none the less, a fascinating place, with leafy walks along the Water of Leith, past St Bernard's Well (see page 116) and up to the magnificent Dean Bridge. Built by Thomas Telford in 1832, this is one of the area's most famous and splendid attractions, with its four arches carrying the road across the water, and its views down into the valley below.

Tron & Dovecote
STENTON

The tranquil atmosphere that pervades the small village of Stenton hides a grim and grisly past. For centuries this quiet, unassuming place played host to the rituals – not uncommon at the time, but certainly barbaric – of witch burning. Here many women, believed to have associations with the Devil, were burnt alive, to the rather macabre pleasure of hundreds of onlookers. Stenton was certainly not the only site of such persecution, but it was one of the last places to surrender these practices and its reputation, whether by natural fascination or commercial contrivance, has remained.

The Tron, which stands on the village green, is a more pleasant relic of Stenton's history. This was used for weighing the wool at the local wool fairs that would take place on and around the village greens, of which Stenton has two. Other features of interest in the village include the Rood Well, an old site of pilgrimage lying at the entrance to the village, and the early nineteenth-century kirk, which incorporates the tower of the original sixteenth-century kirk.

Preston Mill
EAST LINTON

Dean Village was once a concentrated area of one of Lothian's major industries – grain milling – and relics of this can be found all around the outskirts of Edinburgh. At East Linton is one of the best-preserved examples of a grain mill, and here the visitor can witness the ancient methods of milling in one of the oldest working watermills in the country. It was used commercially up until the 1950s, the last of the many mills that were once scattered along the banks of the Tyne. Today, the National Trust for Scotland has recreated the mill as it would have been in its heyday.

Standing beside the River Tyne, this is a romantically picturesque place. The red-pantiled, two-storey sandstone mill dates mainly from the eighteenth century, although parts of it may date from earlier centuries. There are drying kilns, old-fashioned wooden machinery and the essential working waterwheel. The mill even comes complete with its own genuine millpond which, in typical story-book fashion, lies in the shade of apple trees and is home to hosts of ducks.

Seafront
PORTOBELLO

Edinburgh's seafront town takes its name from the first house that was constructed here. Its owner had fought with Admiral Vernon against the Spanish at Peurto Bello in 1739, and on his return to Scotland he settled in this area and built his home here, calling it Portobello. As the town grew, it took its name from the small thatched cottage.

The fine, sandy beach lies three miles east of the city centre, and is popular with both locals and tourists. Like many British seaside towns, Portobello had its heyday in the nineteenth century, and the grand houses that line the streets are typically Georgian and Victorian. After the First World War, the town suffered the fate of many such places, with days of past leisure and wealth. Its pier was destroyed and its popularity waned. Sir Harry Lauder, renowned in music-hall circles, was born here in 1870 when the town was a thriving resort, and this remains one of Portobello's main claims to fame.

Gifford Kirk
GIFFORD

The seventeenth-century village of Gifford lies a short drive away from Edinburgh, and is one of the many pleasant spots on the outskirts of the city. Like most of these places, Gifford has its historical associations. The Reverend John Witherspoon, one of the signatories to the American Declaration of Independence, was born here. On a more romantic note though, Gifford was also home to a known wizard, Sir Hugo Gifford, in the thirteenth century. Sir Hugo's legacy to his home village was a marvellous underground hall, 'Goblin Ha'. The story of Sir Hugo and Goblin Ha caught the imagination of Sir Walter Scott, who incorporated it into his *Marmion*.

Besides the picturesque, whitewashed cottages and church, the village boasts one of the finest estate houses in the area, Yester House. The house was built in 1745, and at the time many of the old village cottages were destroyed and reassembled to lend a more dignified air to Yester House's situation; today the rows of cottages run neatly along the road leading to the large house. The whole village exudes the same air of quiet dignity and careful preservation that characterises so much of Edinburgh's environs.

Village Green & Kirk
DIRLETON

THEY DIED
THAT WE MIGHT LIVE

The dominant feature of Dirleton is undoubtedly the evocative remains of the great thirteenth-century castle (see page 149) that lie on a hill overlooking the village. But the village itself is also worth visiting; it is a typically picturesque place that seems to be largely untouched by time.

The stone cottages are set out along the road, rather than huddled around the two village greens, and most date from the eighteenth and nineteenth centuries. The origins of the village stretch further back than this, though, and it is possible that a village existed here in medieval times, its straight layout one of the features that points to this.

The stone-roofed church, situated on the side of one of the village greens, dates from the seventeenth century. Here on the green a coven of witches were burnt at the stake. It is said that these may even have been the famed witches of North Berwick, although this claim is unsubstantiated.

The Colonies
STOCKBRIDGE

The rise and development of Stockbridge is largely due to Sir Henry Raeburn, one of Scotland's most famous painters. Born here in 1756, when the suburb was no more than a small estate by the Water of Leith, Raeburn's origins were humble. Before he was 30, his fame had spread nation-wide and this, along with his marriage to a wealthy widow, allowed him to buy an estate in his birthplace, which he gradually extended, and later built houses on.

The Colonies, pictured here, were – and still are – some of the most popular residences in the area. They were constructed in 1861 as a trial, which turned out to be successful, and housing schemes along similar lines were subsequently built all over the city. The Colonies were a series of two-storey terraces, each storey comprising its own independent cottage with entrances and gardens on either side.

Today, many of the thatched cottages that characterised the area around Raeburn's time have disappeared, and nineteenth-century tenements are an overriding feature of the modern village. Despite this, Stockbridge is a delightful place to spend time and enjoy the pleasant situation, the street-side cafés and bars, and the antique shops and markets for which the area is now renowned.

Cramond Inn
CRAMOND

The ancient village of Cramond, situated at the mouth of the River Almond to the north-west of Edinburgh, is a major attraction for those seeking to escape from city life. This is not surprising, for Cramond is a veritable haven of tranquillity, enhanced not only by its pleasant situation but also by a fascinating collection of relics, including the remains of a Roman fortification, an old bridge dating from medieval times and a picturesque church with a fifteenth-century tower.

Rows of whitewashed houses lead down a steep hill to the small harbour at the foot of the village. Incongruously nestled amongst the houses, this inn still serves the same purpose as it has since the seventeenth century – to provide good ale and food for those passing through, iron workers and tourists alike. Well preserved and deceptively large, the inn offers a hospitable welcome to those enjoying Cramond's many attractions. Despite Cramond's popularity with visitors, it retains an atmosphere of solitude, and at times can be found perfectly empty, with only the sound of the water below and the wind in the surrounding countryside for company.

Hawes Inn
SOUTH QUEENSFERRY

This historic little town is situated on the shores of the Firth of Forth between the impressive landmarks of the two Forth Bridges. Since ancient times, this has been the crossing point for trips across the Forth, a tradition begun by St Margaret in the eleventh century, who would take the ferry from here to her Palace in Dunfermline. For centuries, the ferries made this trip, until the construction of the bridges provided a quicker and easier access route across the Forth. The town still plays host to an annual ferry fair, however.

South Queensferry retains much of its ancient charm, particularly in the old buildings that line the narrow High Street, including an old Tolbooth. The pub pictured here has its own literary and historic associations. Dating from the late seventeenth century, this was once a coaching inn, and was featured in Scott's *The Antiquary*. As if being mentioned in a novel by

Edinburgh's favourite son wasn't enough, the inn was further immortalised by another of Scotland's great literary heroes, Robert Louis Stevenson. The inn provided the setting for the capture of David Balfour, hero of the novel *Kidnapped*, by his uncle – the start of his adventures.

Village Cross
CULROSS

Walking through the small town of Culross is an unusual experience – a genuine step back in time – for the place has been restored to recall its sixteenth- and seventeenth-century heydays so carefully that it is difficult to imagine that the twentieth century rushes frenetically along just a few minutes away.

At one time, Culross was a large port, carrying on a prosperous trade in a variety of goods, including fish and iron. The Industrial Revolution took its toll here though, and eventually the trade dwindled and the harbour silted up. Culross became, like many other ports, a shadow of its former thriving self. In 1932, the National Trust for Scotland moved in and worked its magic with the town, recreating this beautiful Royal Burgh. It would have been a pity to allow the place to crumble into oblivion, for its origins are truly ancient – it is the site of a religious settlement founded by St Serf as early as the fifth century, with an abbey built over this in the early thirteenth century. The parish church that now stands in Culross does not date from much later than this – *c.* 1300. The original central tower has stood firm through the ravages of time, although the rest of the building was reconstructed in the 1630s.

Forth Road Bridge
SOUTH QUEENSFERRY

The town of South Queensferry is dominated by the two bridges spanning the Firth of Forth at this point, a captivating and dramatic spectacle.

The Forth Road Bridge is one of the longest suspension bridges in the world – indeed at the time of its completion in 1964, it was actually the largest, spanning 1¼ miles to Fife. The towers at either end of the bridge rise to a majestic 156 metres (512 ft) above the water, and the whole bridge used nearly 40,000 tons of metal in its construction, an amazing feat of engineering.

The beauty of this structure can be well appreciated from the shores of the Forth, particularly at night, when the entire bridge is illuminated. But it is the views afforded from the bridge, which allows pedestrian access, that truly complete the spectacle.

The one pity regarding the Road Bridge is that it brought an end to the ferry service that had run since St Margaret's time either across the Firth of Forth from this landing in Queensferry to Fife, or to the island of Inchcolm in the middle. But progress cannot be halted, and commercial ferry services still allow those with the time to experience the pleasure of this ancient crossing.

Forth Rail Bridge
SOUTH QUEENSFERRY

Described as the greatest bridge in Britain, the Forth Rail Bridge is a magnificent feat of nineteenth-century engineering. Carrying a double railway line 1½ miles across the Firth of Forth, this mighty structure reaches 110 metres (360 ft) above the water at its highest point.

The bridge took seven years to build, from 1883 to 1890, and, as often is the case with such mighty works of human endeavour, cost nearly 60 men their lives. It was created by Sir John Fowler and Benjamin Baker and was intended to complete the hitherto inadequate rail network between the south-eastern parts of Scotland with the north. The collapse of the Tay Bridge in 1879 caused the Forth engineers to design their bridge with extreme caution, and the Forth Rail Bridge was created to withstand the worst of conditions, combining solidity with grace.

Together with its neighbour the Forth Road Bridge, this provides one of the most impressive sights in the outskirts of Edinburgh. Both bridges have been carefully maintained so that they may each continue to serve their purpose and represent the pinnacle of engineering achievement of their respective eras.

Index

Act of Union, 10, 68, 150, 163
Adam family, 61, 97
Adam, John, 72, 156
Adam, Robert, 73, 77, 79, 101, 165
Adam, William, 156
Age of Enlightenment, 10
Alexander I, 173
Ann Street, 103
Antonius Pius, Emperor, 164
Apostles, 46
Apprentice Pillar, 56
aqueducts, 123
Argyll aisle, 62
Arnot, Hugo, 172
Art Nouveau, 141
Arthur's Seat, 16, 40, 94, 108, 110, 120, 165
Assembly Rooms, 88
Athena, 126
Athens, 130, 136, 165
bagpipes, 20, 41, 63
Baker, Benjamin, 195
ballet, 31, 42
Balmoral Hotel, 22, 69, 83, 99
Baronial architecture, 96
Bass Rock, 19
Battle of Bannockburn, 25
Battle of Dunbar, 25, 121
Battle of Flodden, 9, 129, 157
Battle of Prestonpans, 114
Battle of Trafalgar, 128
Bell, Alexander Graham, 165
Bing, Rudolf, 31
Blackford Hill, 70
Blackness Castle, 150
Bonnie Prince Charlie, see Stuart, Charles Edward
Bothwell, 25, 145
Boyd, George, 93
Braid Burns, 82
Braid Hills, 82
British Army, 33, 127
Brodie, William, 28, 175
Bronze Age, 14
Bruce, Sir William, 144, 156
Burke and Hare, 28, 166
Burn, William, 146
Burne-Jones, Sir Edward Coley, 50
Burns Monument, 130, 136
Burns, Robert, 62, 136, 140, 174
Caledonian Hotel, 69, 83
Calton Hill, 15, 40, 70, 110, 126, 128, 130, 136, 139, 170
Calvin, John, 171
Calvinism, 9
Cambridge Street, 34
Camera Obscura, 71
cannon, 139

Cannonball House, 92
Canongate Kirk, 55
Canongate Tolbooth, 172
Canongate, 55, 89, 98, 144, 145, 161, 171, 172, 177
Castle Esplanade, 20, 32, 92, 141
Castle Rock, 8, 14, 54
Castlehill, 14, 66, 71, 92, 98, 102, 141, 154
Catholicism, 55
Cavaliers, 25
Chambers, Sir William, 76, 97
Chantrey, 138
Charles I, 9, 46, 61, 62, 157, 160
Charles II, 25, 100, 144, 163
Charlotte Square, 52, 77, 86, 91, 101, 138
China, 113
Choragic Monument of Lysicrates, 130, 136
Christ's Church at the Tron, 53, 94
Cistercian nunnery, 147
City Chambers, 72
City Fathers, 165
City Observatory, 70
City of Edinburgh, 82, 139, 177
Clark, George, 109
classical architecture, 126
Clerk, Sir James and Sir John, 155
Clock Tower, 22, 83
Clow, William and Alexander, 63
Colonies, the, 189
comedy, 20, 31
Commonwealth Games, 81
Corinthian architecture, 58, 97, 136
Costorphine Church, 60
Costorphine Hill, 39
Costorphine, 60
Covenanters, 11, 19, 61, 62, 166
Craig, James, 11, 61, 70, 76, 77, 86, 90, 97, 138
Craigleith, 24
Craigmillar Castle, 152
Cramond, 118, 146, 164, 190
Cromwell, Oliver, 10, 25, 122, 144, 148, 150, 163
Crown Jewels, 163
Crown Office Headquarters, 165
Crystal Palace, 67
Culross, 193
Da Sutri, Domenico, 163
Dalmeny House, 153
Dalmeny Kirk, 49
Dalmeny, 49
Darnley, Lord, 145, 152
David I, 54, 115, 120, 157, 161
David II, 154

De Vaux family, 149
De Wit, Jacob, 145
Deacon Brodie's Tavern, 175
Dean Bridge, 182
Dean Village, 116, 182, 184
Declaration of Independence, 187
Dirleton Castle, 149, 188
Dirleton, 148, 149, 188
'Doors Open Day', 41
Doric architecture, 116
Douglas family, 148
Doyle, Sir Arthur Conan, 134
Dr Jekyll and Mr Hyde, 28, 175
Drummond, George, 86
Duddingston Loch, 114
Duddingston, 114, 152
Dunbar Castle, 25
Dunbar, 25
Dundas, Henry, 91
Dundas, Sir Laurence, 52, 76
Dunfermline, 192
Dunsapie Loch, 108
East Linton, 184
Edinburgh Airport, 38
Edinburgh Astronomical Society, 70
Edinburgh Castle, 14, 20, 25, 29, 32, 33, 40, 47, 54, 66, 87, 99, 148, 154, 162, 163
Edinburgh Episcopalian Church, 46
Edinburgh Festival Fringe, 30, 34
Edinburgh International Conference Centre, 74
Edinburgh International Festival, 10, 20, 30, 31, 32, 36, 42
Edinburgh University, 35, 79, 112, 117, 130, 167
Edinburgh Zoo, 39
Edward I, 25
Edward II, 25
Edward the Confessor, 120
Elizabeth I, 9, 171
Episcopacy, 9, 53, 61, 62
Esk Valley, 56
Eyebroughty, 24
Falkirk, 123
Federation of Master Builders, 134
'ferm toun', 180
Festival Theatre, 35
Fidra Island, 24
Fife, 109, 110, 118, 194
First World War, 36, 39, 141, 186
Firth of Forth, 15, 19, 40, 82, 109, 110, 116, 120, 128, 146, 150, 156, 164, 173, 192, 194, 195
fishing, 110, 121
Floral Clock, 107

Forrest, George, 113
Forrester, Sir Adam, 60
Forth and Clyde Canal, 123
Forth Estuary, 118
Forth Rail Bridge, 192, 195
Forth Road Bridge, 192, 194
Fowke, Francis, 67
Fowler, Sir John, 195
Frazer, Major Andrew, 52
Free Church of Scotland, 52
Gainsborough, 153
Geddes, Patrick, 71, 102
'Geordie Boyd's Mud Brig', 93
George IV Bridge, 88
George IV, 138
George Square, see Charlotte Square
George Street, 52, 77, 86, 91, 101, 138
George VI, 115
Georgian architecture, 11, 76, 86, 91, 96, 97, 181, 186
Georgian House, the, 101
ghosts, 11, 28, 72, 144
Gifford, 187
Gifford, Sir Hugo, 187
Gillespie, James, 176
Gladstone's Land, 160
Glasgow, 123
'Glasshouse Experience', 113
Gledstane, Thomas, 160
Glyndebourne Opera, 31
'Goblin Ha', 187
'Goose-Pie House', 102
'Gowrie Conspiracy', 149
Gowrie, Earl of, 149
Graham, James Gillespie, 90
Grassmarket, 11, 28, 34, 92, 166
Gray, John, 132
Great Disruption, 52
Great Michael, 109
'Green Men', 50
Greenhouse Place, 42
Greyfriars Bobby, 60, 132
Greyfriars Kirkyard, 9, 61, 132
Guardian Royal Exchange, 91
Guest, Crispin, 21
Haddington, 50, 147
Haig, Field Marshall, 141
Halyburton family, 149
Hamilton, Thomas, 165
hammerbeam roof, 53, 68
Hanover Street, 138
Hawes Inn, 192
Heart of Midlothian, 168
Henry VIII, 9
Hepburn, Sir John, 33
Heriot Row, 167

Hertford, Earl of, 144, 152
High Kirk of St Giles, 9, 47, 53, 62, 63, 68, 129, 168, 171, 172
High Street, 43, 62, 63, 68, 72, 92, 98, 129, 168
Highland cattle, 38
Highlands, 16, 18, 167
Holmes, Sherlock, 134
Holyrood Abbey, 8, 55, 87, 115, 120, 161
Holyrood Park, 15, 16, 57, 80, 81, 108, 114, 115, 120
'Honest Toun', 121
'Honours of Scotland', 163
Hopetoun House, 156
Hopetoun, Earls of, 156
Hungary, 120
Huntly House Museum, 177
Hygieia, 116
Inchcolm Abbey, 173
Inchcolm Island, 173, 194
Incorporation of Baxters, 182
Incorporation of Hammermen, 177
Industrial Revolution, 10, 193
Ingliston, 38
International Holography Exhibition, 71
Inveresk Lodge Gardens, 181
Inveresk, 121, 181
Inverleith, 112, 113
Jacobean, 146
Jacobites, 19, 157
James I, 19, 157
James II, 55, 160
James III, 160
James IV, 109, 144, 157, 160, 163
James V, 145, 148, 152, 157, 160, 163
James VI (James I of England), 9, 79, 114, 162
James, VII, 63
John the Baptist, 46
Kemp, George Meikle, 135
Kidnapped, 192
King Harold, 120
King Herod, 43
Knights of the Order of the Thistle, 55, 63
Knox, John, 9, 145, 171
Knox, Robert, 166
Lady Stair's House, 174
Laing, Gerald Ogilvie, 134
Lamb, 24
Lanarkshire, 123
Lauder, Sir Harry, 186
Lauriston Castle, 146
Law Courts, 68

Law, John, 146
Lawnmarket, 93, 98, 100, 174
Leith Walk, 112
Leith, 57, 70, 118, 122, 170
lighthouses, 19, 24
Linlithgow, 157
Little, Clement, 79
London, 10, 42, 89, 134
Lord Lyon King of Arms, 129
Lorimer, Sir Robert, 63
Lothian Road, 36, 48, 58
Lothian, 11, 16, 184
Louis XIII, 33
Malcolm III, 54, 120, 154, 162
Marchmont, 96
Marlin's Wynd, 53
Marmion, 187
Marquis of Montrose, 129
Martyr's Monument, 61
Mary King's Close, 72
Mary of Guise, 171
Mary, Queen of Scots, 9, 25, 122,
    129, 145, 149, 152, 157, 160,
    162, 171
Meadowbank Stadium, 80, 81
Meadows International Exhibition,
    139
Meadows, the, 96, 117
Medieval, 46, 60, 62, 87, 110, 129,
    190
Melville Monument, 91
Mercat Cross, 129
Merlion, Walter, 53
Military Tattoo, 20, 32
Mill's Mount Battery, 40, 92
mill-pond, 184
milling communities, 116, 118,
    123, 182, 184
Monastery of the Holy Rood, 161
Moray Place, 90
Moray, Earl of, 90
Morrison Street, 74
Mound, the, 93, 102, 106, 138, 140
Murray, Patrick, 43
Murrayfield Stadium, 80
Museum of Childhood, 43
musicals, 20, 31
Musselburgh, 121
Mylne's Court, 100
Mylne, James, 103
Mylne, Robert, 100
Napoleon Bonaparte, 153
Napoleonic Wars, 126
Nasmyth, Alexander, 58
National Covenant, 9, 61, 177
National Gallery of Scotland, 78,
    106
National Monument, 126, 130

National Portrait Gallery, 136
National Trust for Scotland, 181,
    184, 193
Nelson Monument, 15, 40, 128
Nelson, Admiral Horatio, 128
Neo-classical architecture, 73
New Town, 10, 15, 22, 41, 47, 52,
    61, 70, 86, 87, 90, 91, 93, 94, 96,
    97, 101, 112, 135, 138, 167, 182
Newhaven, 109, 118
Nicolson Street, 35
Nor' Loch, 93, 94, 106
North Berwick, 24, 188
North Bridge, 22, 53, 94, 97
North British Hotel, see Balmoral
    Hotel
Old Observatory, 70
Old Royal High School, 165
Old Tolbooth, 98, 168, 192
Old Town Information Centre, 53
Old Town Renewal Trust, 41
Old Town, 10, 15, 20, 28, 41, 62,
    66, 68, 72, 73, 83, 86, 87, 88, 93,
    94, 96, 97, 98, 99, 100, 102, 106,
    138, 167
One o'Clock Gun, 40, 128
opera, 20, 30, 35, 42
Osbourne, Fanny, 167
Outlook Tower, 41, 92
Palace of Holyroodhouse, 89, 98,
    100, 138, 144, 145
Palmerston Place, 46, 47
Paolozzi, Sir Edouardo, 134
Paris Exhibition, 133
Parliament House, 68
Parliament Square, 68
Parthenon, 126
Penicuik, 155
Pentland Hills, 18, 116, 155, 180
'People's Story', the, 172
Picardy Place, 134
Picardy Regiment, 33
Pinkie House, 121
Pitt the Younger, 91
Plague, the, 72
Playfair, William, 70, 78, 79, 126,
    130
Playhouse Theatre, 42
'Pontius Pilate's Bodyguard', see
    Royal Scots Regiment
pop concerts, 42
Pope Julius II, 163
Portobello, 186
Pre-Raphaelites, 50, 62
Presbyterianism, 9, 47, 51
Preston Mill, 184
Primrose, Viscount, 174
Prince Albert, 115, 120

Princes Street Gardens, 29, 69, 83,
    94, 99, 102, 106, 107, 117, 127,
    133, 135, 140
Princes Street, 21, 22, 40, 48, 69,
    73, 78, 83, 86, 93, 99, 106, 112,
    127, 135, 138, 140, 170
Prosecution Service, 165
Protestantism, 55, 171
Public Record Office, 77
Queen Margaret, 157
Queen Street, 86
Raeburn, Sir Henry, 78, 153, 189
Ramsay Garden, 102
Ramsay, Allan, 61, 102, 107, 127,
    140
Ramsden, Harry, 109
Randolph, Thomas, 121, 162
Raphael, 78
Reformation, 47, 62, 161, 173
Regents Road, 136
Register House, 73
Reid, Robert, 68, 77
Rembrandt, 78
Restoration, 10, 147, 163
Reynolds, 153
Rhind, Bernie, 127
River Almond, 118, 164, 190
River Esk, 121, 181
River Tyne, 184
Rizzio, 145, 149, 152
Robert the Bruce, 121, 163
Roman fort, 164, 190
Romanesque architecture, 49
Rood Well, 183
Roseberry, Earls of, 153
Ross Fountain, 29, 133
Ross Open Air Theatre, 29
Ross, Daniel, 133
Rosslyn Chapel, 56
Roundheads, 25
Royal Bank of Scotland, 52, 76
Royal Botanic Garden, 112, 113
Royal Charter, 79
Royal College of Physicians, 112
Royal Engineers, 52, 67
Royal Exchange, 72
Royal Highland Show, 38
Royal Mile, 8, 41, 47, 53, 55, 66,
    87, 88, 89, 92, 94, 98, 129, 132,
    136, 144, 160, 170, 172, 175,
    176
Royal Museum of Scotland, 67
Royal Observatory, 70
Royal Proclamation, 129
Royal Scots Greys, 33, 127, 174
Royal Scottish Academy, 106, 138
Ruthven family, 149
Salisbury Crags, 15, 94, 128

Scotch Whisky Heritage Centre, 66
Scott Monument, 99, 135
Scott, Sir George Gilbert, 47
Scott, Sir Walter, 110, 163, 174,
    187, 192
Scottish Agricultural Museum, 38
Scottish National Orchestra, 36
Scottish Parliament, 68, 126
Scottish Reformed Church, 171
Second New Town, 90
Second World War, 10, 139
Septimus Severus, Emperor, 164
Sheeps Heid Inn, 114
shipbuilding, 109, 122
Short, Maria Theresa, 71
Signet Library, 68
Simpson, Dr James, 127
Slum Clearances, 100
Smith, James, 55
South Loch, 117
South Queensferry, 150, 153, 156,
    192, 194, 195
sports, 80
Spylaw, 176
St Andrew and St George's
    Church, 52, 77
St Andrew's Square, 52, 76, 77, 86,
    91, 101, 138
St Andrew, 54, 163
St Anthony's Chapel, 57, 120
St Baldred, 19
St Bernard's Well, 116, 182
St Bernard of Clairvaux, 116
St Clair, William, 56
St Columba, 54
St Cuthbert's Kirk, 48, 58
St George's Church, 77
St Giles Cathedral, see High Kirk
    of St Giles
St James's Court, 34
St John's Kirk, 48, 133
St Margaret's Loch, 108, 115, 120
St Margaret's Chapel, 54, 154
St Margaret, 54, 58, 120, 192, 194
St Mary's Church (Haddington), 50
St Mary's Episcopalian Cathedral,
    46, 47
St Michael's Church (Linlithgow),
    157
St Ninian, 54
St Serf, 193
stained glass, 53, 54, 55
Stair, Earl of, 174
Stair, Lady, 174
Stark, William, 68
Steell, Sir John, 135, 140
Stenton, 183
Stevenson House, 147

Stevenson, Robert Louis, 15, 18,
    24, 167, 174, 175, 180, 192
Stevenson, Thomas, 180
Stewart, Dugald, 130, 136
Stirling Castle, 149
Stockbridge, 103, 189
Stone Age, 14
Stuart, Charles Edward, 89, 92,
    114, 115, 154, 157
Supreme Court of Scotland, 68
Swanston, 18, 180
Tantallon Castle, 148
Tay Bridge, 195
Tea Table Miscellany, 140
Telford, Thomas, 182
Temple of Theseus, 165
tenements, 96
The Antiquary, 192
The Gentle Shepherd, 140
theatre, 31
Thistle Chapel, 63
Tolbooth St John's, 92
Town College, 79
Traverse Theatre, 34
Treasure Island, 24
Tron Kirk, see Christ's Church at
    the Tron
Union Canal, 123
Usher Hall, 36
Usher, Andrew, 36
Van Dycke, 78
Vernon, Admiral, 186
Victoria Street, 88
Victorian Edinburgh Exhibition, 71
Victorian, 113, 114, 182, 186
volcanoes, 14, 15, 19
Walker, Barbara and Mary, 47
Wallace, William, 54
Warrender, Sir George, 96
Wars of Independence, 162
Water of Leith, 116, 182, 189
Waterloo Bridge, 170
Waverley Market, 21
Waverley Station, 21, 22, 69, 94
West Bow, 88
West Register House, 77
whisky, 66
White Horse Close, 89
Wilkins, William, 153
witches, 28, 141, 183, 188
Witherspoon, Reverend John, 187
Writers' Museum, the, 174
Yellowcraig, 24
Yester House, 187